THE WORK OF ART

**A Summary of the Economic
Importance of the Arts in Britain**

PSI reports on the Economic Importance of the Arts:

THE ECONOMIC IMPORTANCE OF THE ARTS IN BRITAIN
John Myerscough
256 pages 241 x 171 mm 0/85374/354/1 Hardback £19.95

THE ECONOMIC IMPORTANCE OF THE ARTS IN GLASGOW
John Myerscough
288 pages 210 x 144 mm 0/85374/420/9 Paperback £5.95

THE ECONOMIC IMPORTANCE OF THE ARTS
IN MERSEYSIDE
John Myerscough
108 pages 210 x 144 mm 0/85374/429/4 Paperback £5.95

THE ECONOMIC IMPORTANCE OF THE ARTS IN IPSWICH
John Myerscough
224 pages 210 x 144 mm 0/85374/430/0 Paperback £5.95

The above reports are available from all good bookshops, or in the case of difficulty directly from The Publications Department, Policy Studies Institute, 100 Park Village East, London NW1 3SR.

THE WORK OF ART

A Summary of the Economic Importance of the Arts In Britain

Peter Rodgers, based on *The Economic Importance of the Arts in Britain* (PSI, 1988) by John Myerscough

Calouste Gulbenkian Foundation
Policy Studies Institute

PSI Publications are obtainable from all good bookshops, or by visiting the Institute at: 100 Park Village East, London NW1 3SR (01-387 2171).

Sales representation: Pinter Publishers Ltd.

Individual and Bookshop orders to: Marston Book Services Ltd, PO Box 87, Oxford, OX4 1LB.

A CIP catalogue record of this book is available from the British Library.

ISBN 0 903319 446 Calouste Gulbenkian Foundation

ISBN 0 85374 427 0 Policy Studies Institute

Laserset by AL Publishing Services, London W4

Printed by Bourne Offset Ltd., Iver, Bucks.

FOREWORD

This shortened version of John Myerscough's report *The Economic Importance of the Arts in Britain* is published six months after the main report. This affords a rare opportunity to comment on the reaction to the report. The press has responded with many column inches, and with very favourable reviews - "likely to set the agenda for arts for the next ten years". It is now one of PSI's best ever selling publications.

However, a few words of caution are in order. The report's arguments are sophisticated, but more important, they are inter-dependent. The impact and validity of the report is lessened if any one of its arguments is used in isolation. Whilst some sectors of the national economy may provide more impressive results regarding job creation, development of ancillary industries or customer spending, very few, if any, can offer such a broad range of reasons for encouraging investment - jobs, overseas earnings, revitalisation of urban areas, tourism, and indirect customer spending. Moreover the report reveals that a wide cross-section of the public believes in the importance of the arts, and recognises their value in creating and maintaining a good quality of life.

In some quarters worries have been expressed about too close a relationship between the economy and the arts, believing that this relationship undermines the true value of the arts, that is, the aesthetic and the social. This misses the point, for the main thrust of the report's argument is that it is indeed these very same values which make the arts so economically successful. Increasingly the view is held that developing resources which create a good quality of life makes good economic sense. To demonstrate the economic power of the arts in no way diminishes their other values. The arts coin has two sides, and it is hoped that this study will imprint a head as well as a tail on that coin.

Iain Reid
Assistant Director, Arts
UK Branch
Calouste Gulbenkian Foundation

Contents

INTRODUCTION

The arts in Britain are a major sector of the economy. They are comparable in their importance to the national economy with such giants as vehicles or fuel and power; they are vital export earners, an important source of employment and a power for good in regional regeneration.

This report has been written to establish the significance of the arts to the British economy: directly in earnings and jobs, and indirectly as a stimulus to ancillary industries, including tourism. The success of cities in the future will depend on how well they build up their services and amenities. The arts play a vital role in helping to promote a particular place as civilised and interesting - somewhere people will want to live and to locate businesses.

The arts are a service industry and we live in an era of industrial restructuring in which services are growing in importance, especially in areas such as finance, information, travel and entertainment. Technology is at the same time rechannelling the media into new forms, from video to satellite TV, increasing the number of outlets for the arts.

The report, of which this is a summary, draws extensively on three regional studies of Glasgow, Merseyside and Ipswich, which are published separately. Glasgow more than anywhere else demonstrated the power which a vibrant artistic life has to reinvigorate a city, to attract and keep talent, and to help persuade industrialists to locate their businesses in the region. It is no coincidence that Glasgow's growing cultural pride has coincided with a re-emerging civic and business self-confidence proved by its designation as European City of Culture 1990.

In different ways the experiences of Merseyside and Ipswich also make clear the vital role of the arts not just in providing direct jobs but also in laying the groundwork for a still elusive economic recovery - in the case of Merseyside - or continued growth in the case of Ipswich.

The issues now should be not whether the arts have a significant economic importance, but how great is it, how can it be further encouraged and exploited, and how should arts policy be related to wider economic aims? Realisation of the wider importance of the arts to Britain has stimulated new willingness to contribute financially, both from private sector companies and from other bodies such as local authorities.

This summary, of a much longer report[*], is necessarily complex. Chapter 1 begins with a brief definition of the arts market and a description of the scope of the work done for the main report, and the three regional surveys. This is followed by some number crunching, to lay foundations for the rest of the work. Chapter 2 looks at the number of customers for concerts, theatres, museums and galleries and discovers that there has been healthy growth recently. It also looks at the amount of money spent by arts customers. Chapter 3 looks at the arts market in several regions of the country and shows that arts customers cover a much wider social mix than many people probably imagine. Chapter 4 looks at the growth in attendance at arts events and the rise of electrical home entertainment. Contrary to popular supposition, live events have not suffered from declining audiences in the face of competition from TV and video in the home.

Chapter 5 is the first of several which take a look at the wider and indirect influence of the arts on the economy (whereas Chapter 2 concentrated simply on direct returns from theatres, museums and galleries). In Chapter 6 we trace the economic effects of the arts beyond the performances, events and artifacts produced by the mainstream industry. The arts are a magnet for people who will also spend money on food, shopping, accommodation and souvenirs. Chapters 5 and 6 together are the basis for a new estimate which claims that the total of sales and other income accruing to the arts in Britain is at least £10 billion per annum.

Chapter 7 looks at the contributions of grants and subsidies to the arts followed by an examination in Chapter 8 of how the arts compare as a cost effective method of job creation with others that the government is trying. It concludes that they are better than most. To set the statistical framework Chapter 8 begins with an account of the numbers of jobs directly provided by the arts industry in Britain, and concludes that it will reach 550,000 by 1990. Chapter 9 suggests how the benefits of plans for investing in the arts can be analysed. Chapter 10 starts by showing that the export performance of the arts is better than manufacturing industry and fourth in the league table among so called invisible exporters, those who do not sell physical

---

[*] The Economic Importance of the Arts in Britain, PSI, London, 1988

products. It ranks behind banking, travel and shipping and ahead of civil aviation. The rest of the chapter is a study of the contribution of the arts to tourism. Overseas tourism specifically attributable to the arts earned Britain nearly £1.5 billion in 1984.

Chapter 11 is significant for policy-makers because it shows, on the basis of surveys, that public opinion generally favours current levels of spending of tax revenue on the arts. There was wide support for the arts among all social classes, and simply no backing for the view that the arts are of value to only a small minority. Chapter 12 considers the value of the arts in urban renewal, and the way they can reanimate city life. Chapter 13 examines the closely related subject of the arts and business. Senior executives clearly believe that a strong cultural infrastructure is a positive asset for a region, like its roads or its telecommunications. Chapter 14 draws together the threads of the report and sets out suggestions for action to achieve the economic expansion of the arts by central government, public agencies, local authorities, business, tourist and arts organisations; and Chapter 15 describes the strategies suggested to achieve this growth.

Finally, a word about the origins of the report. The Policy Studies Institute was originally approached by the UK Branch of the Calouste Gulbenkian Foundation to discuss the feasibility of a research programme on the economic importance of the arts in Britain, and to draw up a possible research brief. The brief was agreed and the research programme was formally commissioned by the Foundation and the Office of Arts and Libraries. Further financial support was provided from national sources by the Museums and Galleries Commission, the Arts Council of Great Britain and the Crafts Council. A search for appropriate regions willing to provide the necessary finance led to the establishment of three regional case studies: the Merseyside study was part of a larger commission by Merseyside County Council, Merseyside Arts (with the help of the Granada Foundation), Merseyside Development Corporation and the Commission of the European Communities; in Ipswich, on the initiative of Eastern Arts, finance was provided by Suffolk County Council, Babergh, Mid-Suffolk and Suffolk Coastal District Councils and by Ipswich Borough Council; the Glasgow study was commissioned by Glasgow Action, the Glasgow District Council and the Scottish Arts Council with a contribution from the Greater Glasgow Tourist Board.

CHAPTER 1:
WHAT ARE THE ARTS?

The arts are not easy to define as a separate sector of the economy. The boundaries for the study have been chosen conservatively.

There are difficulties in defining 'the arts' for a study like this which are compounded by the 'overlapping' of artistic experiences - for example the music listened to at home on tape, disc or video, and live in a concert hall. Which forms should be included as constituting the arts sector of the economy?

The study has adopted a broad definition of the arts, but not so broad that it can be accused of exaggerating the contribution to the economy. It includes public and private sector activities, and covers museums and galleries, theatres and concerts, creative artists, community arts and the crafts. It also casts the net wider to include the screen industries, broadcasting, the art trade, book publishing and the music industries, all of which have a large arts content. Architecture, advertising and design, amateur organisations and education are among the important activities which have been excluded. By widening the definition it would have been possible to make bigger but more controversial claims.

The definition of the arts used for the main report was 'those endeavours in which the development and conveyance of an original artistic idea or experience to the public is the primary purpose, whether to improve or to entertain'. Where the artistic element, however important, was secondary to another aim - for example in advertising or design - then the activity concerned was wholly excluded.

It should be no surprise that there were difficulties in interpreting this distinction consistently. Transport museums, which have only tenuous links with the arts, are included because they are organisationally part of the museums and galleries. On the other hand, artist designed ties, to take a highly specialised example, would be excluded because they are part of the fashion industry rather than arts and crafts.

The study does emphasise the great value of the contribution made by workers with artistic training who are employed in wide areas of the manufacturing and service industries. Artistic ideas often have a vital role where words or presentational skills come into play. But there has been no attempt to include these other industries in estimates of the income producing and job creation roles of the arts.

Economic impact studies of the arts have in the past been criticised for exaggerating positive benefits, ignoring negative ones, using suspect relationships, failing to consider alternative uses of public money and measuring gains which are illusory because they are only a shift to one area at the expense of another. Careful efforts have been made throughout the main report and the three regional studies to try to avoid such pitfalls.

As well as drawing on nationally available statistics, the three regional studies and the main report relied on 24 original surveys covering arts organisations, customers, local residents and business executives in an attempt to establish how people spent their money, where and why they were spending it, and what they thought of the arts. The surveys were used to collect a great deal of basic business information about the arts and related industries which has allowed a more accurate picture to be drawn of the arts as an economic activity. There were a large number of special inquiries, such as those which helped establish the value of overseas earnings. These foreign trade results are so important that they should be regularly updated.

A distinction is sometimes made between the high arts which require public subsidy to remain creatively pure, and the market sector which is charged with supplying a 'debased' mass culture. But nowadays there is a great overlap and indeed a cross-fertilisation between the two, financially and creatively. This report therefore includes in the arts the revenues of pop concerts as well as of symphony orchestras, and West End hits as well as experimental plays.

This report is most closely concerned with the market for cultural events and attractions outside the home, such as museums, galleries, theatres and concerts. It also takes into account the economic importance of arts enjoyed in one way or another in the home and the contribution to the arts of broadcasting, publishing and the record industry. It is important to remember that different ways of approaching the same arts may compete for spending yet at the same time reinforce each other. For example, a video may substitute for a visit to a show. It can just as easily be an incentive to buy a ticket actually to visit it, or become a memento afterwards. For performing artists, contact with a live audience is important, but so are the financial rewards of studio work, which keep the wolf from the door and are sometimes exceptionally lucrative.

Paintings are sold to public galleries and private collectors alike, but they are also reproduced commercially in large numbers. The many channels through which artistic ideas and performances reach the public inside and outside the home make for an exceptionally complex market.

CHAPTER 2:
THE MARKET FOR EVENTS AND ATTRACTIONS

After the economic recession of the early 1980s, which hit the arts as well as other aspects of British life, growth has resumed. Total consumer spending on the performed arts of the theatre and concert hall, together with admissions to museums and galleries, amounted to £433 million in 1985/86. There are more facilities, more performances of all kinds and bigger audiences for the arts than there were ten years ago.

By the mid-1980s most of the arts were trading at higher levels than a decade earlier. Museums and galleries had the biggest market share, measured by the number of attendances at 73 million; the figure for theatres and concerts was 49 million. Cinema kept its position as the most popular evening entertainment though it had contracted by more than half over the previous decade.

Museums and Galleries

The 19 national museums and galleries with over 50 sites between them were dominated by London, where the British Museum (4.1 million) and the National Gallery (3.2 million) were among the top draws in Britain, second only to Blackpool Pleasure Beach. In total the local authority museums and galleries were not far behind the national organisations, with 22.6 million attendances at 750 facilities. The 906 independent museums, including 21 run by universities, and such projects as the Beaulieu Motor Museum (488,000), were in the same league, with almost 20 million visits. This group has been expanding, and ranges from big commercial organisations to a host of small local museums, often run by volunteers. This total is completed by temporary loan exhibitions, held in galleries, museums and arts centres, with 5.4 million attendances.

Estimates by the English Tourist Board suggest that growth in attendances was 6 per cent overall from 1976 to 1985. Figures for the national museums and galleries show an uneven picture, growing massively in the 1970s, declining a little in the early 1980s and resuming growth from 1983 to 1985, though remaining below the 1977 peak until 1987. New national museums, such as Film and Photography which opened in Bradford in 1983, may explain some of the recent growth.

For local authority museums, evidence from Glasgow, Ipswich and Merseyside suggests that the trend is slightly upwards, though this may not be true elsewhere. As for the independent museums, their expansion - two fifths were founded between 1971 and 1984 - must have been a boost to museum and gallery attendances but competition between them is increasingly severe.

Because some museums and galleries charge and others do not, the sales totals look comparatively modest. Admission charges yielded £18 million, of which £1 million to £2 million was at national museums and galleries, £2 million to £4 million at local authority establishments and £11 million at other (mainly independent) museums. Temporary exhibitions in London raised £4 million.

Table 2.1   Attendance at theatres and concerts, 1984/85

Millions and numbers

	Attendance (millions)	Facilities (numbers)	Performances (numbers)
Theatres			
London's West End (a)	10.0	51(b)	16,193
Opera houses and number-one receiving theatres outside London (c)	5.7	23	5,290
Producing theatres	4.4	52	15,250
Other theatres outside London	14.1	166	34,540
Small venues and arts centres	3.1	311	19,710
Sub-total	37.3	603	90,983
Film theatres	0.9	51	..
Concerts			
Symphony concerts	2.5	152	1,720
Chamber orchestras, ensembles, recitals	2.2	..	7,300
Pop, rock, jazz and folk	5.7	..	3,900
Sub-total	10.4	..	12,920
Total	*48.6*	..	*103,903*

Source: Facts 2: British Theatre Directory; Arts Council of Great Britain; Theatrical Management Association.
(a) Includes national companies (drama, opera and dance) operating 7 auditoria with 1.99 million attendance in London; also includes one subsidised producing theatre, the Royal Court.
(b) The National Theatre and Royal Shakespeare Company operate 5 theatres in London making a total of 51 auditoria in London's West End.
(c) Includes an estimated 2 million attendances at Arts-Council-funded opera, dance and drama tours.

Theatres and Concerts

There were 49 million tickets sold for live professional arts events in 1984/85 (see Table 2.1), excluding 14 to 16 million attendances at amateur shows and 2 to 3 million amateur concerts by schools, colleges and local societies. Theatre attracted the sale of 38 million seats compared with 10 million for concerts. London's West End theatre audiences alone totalled 10 million including 2 million seats at performances by the national drama, opera and dance companies in the capital, the rest of the tickets being sold at independently managed West End theatres. Not surprisingly, musicals won the biggest audience share.

Opera and dance had a national audience of 2.4 million, of which half was included in the West End total and the rest was at opera houses outside London such as the Grand Theatre, Leeds (Opera North) and the Theatre Royal, Glasgow (Scottish Opera), as well as at major provincial 'receiving' theatres (those that receive touring companies). In addition to opera and dance, these big theatres attracted a 4.5 million audience to touring plays, musicals, pantomimes and other shows.

The main drama seasons outside central London were provided by 52 Arts Council funded 'producing' theatres (those that produce plays, not simply receive touring companies) with an audience of 4.4 million, while another 166 provincial theatres sold 14 million tickets for a wide variety of events. These included seaside summer show theatres (of which 13 were privately owned), more than a hundred local authority theatres presenting anything from drama to variety, and a range of independent theatres.

At the other end of the scale, more than 300 small venues and arts centres drew an audience of 3 to 4 million. Average attendance for small-scale touring drama funded by the Arts Council was only 132 per performance. The venues used often have no regular programming.

As with the rest of the arts, theatre and concert markets have been expanding. For example, the West End sold 10.8 million tickets in 1985, 28 per cent more than in 1981. Research for the Society of West End Theatre, by City University, shows that a major reason for the increase was the attendance of tourists from abroad. The flood of visitors to London brought a 68 per cent growth in ticket sales to foreign tourists between 1982 and 1985. Sales to Londoners grew by a respectable 15 per cent, but British visitors to London bought 4 per cent fewer tickets. There was a significant rise in the number of people going to the theatre, as fewer tickets went to regulars. There was also a sharp rise in the number of performances so that the average audience for each fell slightly.

Outside London's West End a fall in ticket sales at Arts Council funded 'producing' theatres was reversed between 1982 and 1986, when there was a 12 per cent increase. National drama companies bottomed out in 1981/82 and producing theatres elsewhere a year later. Not only did the number of performances rise, but there was also an increase in audience size so that by the mid-1980s both the West End and the subsidised theatres were attracting record audiences. For much of the rest of the theatrical world the data are not good enough to establish trends confidently, though a Mintel survey showed a rise from 37 million to 39 million in the nationwide theatre audience from 1981 to 1984.

Opera sold slightly more tickets in the 1980s than in the 1970s, mainly because there were more performances. Dance fell from a high in the late 1970s until 1983/84 but began to recover over the next couple of years.

The new estimate of spending on theatre tickets has been compiled from a number of sources, including West End theatre and Arts Council statistics. Sample information on ticket sales, some taken

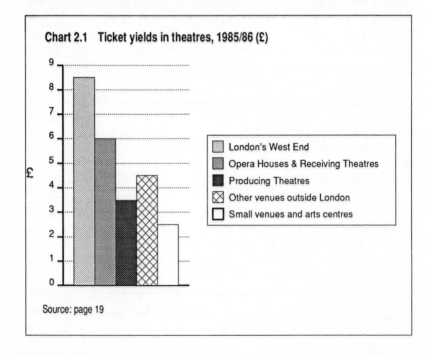

Chart 2.1   Ticket yields in theatres, 1985/86 (£)

Legend:
- London's West End
- Opera Houses & Receiving Theatres
- Producing Theatres
- Other venues outside London
- Small venues and arts centres

Source: page 19

from the three regional case studies, has been used to fill in the gaps. The conclusion is that total box office takings, including VAT, came to £207 million in 1985/86.

Live music's audience of 10.4 million splits equally between classical and popular concerts. A very rough estimate for popular music audiences was made on the basis of a sample which showed that over the period of a year 12 per cent of the adult population attended a popular concert.

However, better statistics were available for symphony concert audiences. The main concert halls drew 84 per cent of the 2.5 million total. Symphony concerts have become more popular, with a rise of a quarter in the decade to 1984, and of nearly two fifths in London, though there was a low point at the beginning of the decade. The market widened when the Barbican Hall opened in London, though the size of the average audience fell. Chamber orchestras, ensembles and recitalists, using the major halls and a large number of other non-specialist venues, added a further 2.2 million ticket sales, which amounts to a total of approximately 5.7 million attendances.

Using similar methods for the theatre estimates, spending on concert tickets appears to have been £49 million, of which £30 million went to jazz, folk, rock and pop concerts and £19.5 million to classical concerts. Naturally, the big symphony orchestras drew the most money, taking £13 million of the serious music revenues.

Cinemas
Attendances have fallen rapidly from the mid-1950s, a trend noticed in most industrialised countries. However in the UK by 1982 the market had levelled out and in 1985 and 1986 there was an encouraging recovery so that the cinema may now have begun a new era. According to the Central Statistical Office, £125 million worth of tickets were bought in 1985/86, (see Chart 2.2).

Other Spending
A wave of openings of small arts centres in the early 1980s suggests that attendance at these mixed programme venues is probably expanding, though there are no statistics to prove it.

The English Tourist Board estimated that visits to historic buildings rose at least 16 per cent in the decade to 1985, including newly opened attractions, though there was a dip during the depression in the economy between 1978 and 1982. The ETB estimates an average £1.04 admission price at historic buildings which charge, producing revenue of nearly £34 million.

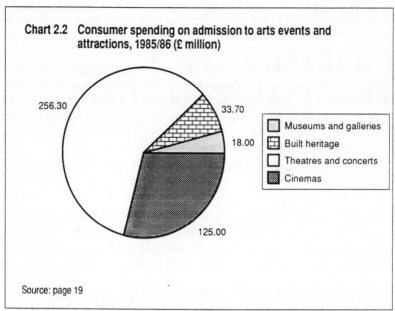

Chart 2.2 Consumer spending on admission to arts events and attractions, 1985/86 (£ million)

256.30

33.70

18.00

125.00

Museums and galleries
Built heritage
Theatres and concerts
Cinemas

Source: page 19

The conclusion is that there has been healthy growth recently in most fields of the arts outside the home. Total spending in 1985 emerges from the new estimates as £433 million, well over half of it at theatres and concerts.

CHAPTER 3:
REGIONAL AND OTHER DIFFERENCES IN THE ARTS MARKET

Arts are not a minority interest. They reach out to two thirds of the adult population. Here we look at regional and other differences and ask how many individuals visit the arts - rather than how many tickets are sold.

Not surprisingly because London is a magnet for regional, national and international audiences, it was also the dominant force in theatre, concerts, museums and galleries, accounting for over a third of all attendances. London has a particularly high concentration of ticket sales for symphony concerts (45 per cent) and opera (57 per cent), and three times as much of the market as would be expected from its share of Britain's population.

Although ticket sales are much more uneven across the rest of Britain, two of the three regional study areas also had above their share, measured against local population. Glasgow was particularly successful with 4.9 per cent of the museum and gallery market, 3.5 per cent of the theatre and concert market and only 2.9 per cent of the population. Ipswich, with the Wolsey Theatre and Aldeburgh nearby, was ahead on theatres and concerts though average on museums and galleries. Merseyside was the only one of the three with a lower than average theatre and concert attendance, though it had a higher score for museums and galleries.

Tourists made up the largest part of the London audience: local residents were in a minority, except at symphony concerts and the Royal Opera House. Outside London local residents formed four fifths of the market for concerts and theatre and between one third and two thirds at museums and galleries. Some particularly celebrated institutions such as the Burrell Collection in Glasgow reversed this pattern, drawing more of their support from outside the region than from within it.

Table 3.1   **Residents, day visitors and tourists in the arts markets for selected regions**

Percentages

	Glasgow	Merseyside	Ipswich	London
Museums and galleries: percentage of attendances by:				
Residents	56	65	36	29
Day Visitors	19	20	34	27
Tourists	25	15	30	44
Theatres and concerts: percentage of attendance by:				
Residents	85	87	83	39
Day Visitors	13	9	9	21
Tourists	2	4	8	40

Source: Facts About the Arts 2, PSI, London, 1986.

By social class, museums and galleries had a wider attendance than theatres and concerts in the three study regions, though the pattern was not uniform. Musicals and pantomimes helped lift the proportion of classes C2, D and E in the Glasgow receiving theatres to 33 per cent, while small venues in country towns around Ipswich drew a remarkable 45 per cent of their audiences from the same group.

By sex, the overall figures for museum and gallery attendance were evenly balanced, but this masked a male preference for science and transport and a female preference for art. Women dominated theatre and concert audiences in the three regional studies, with the extreme case Glasgow's 75 per cent female opera and ballet audiences. Women also predominated in London, except at the Royal Opera House and at symphony concerts.

By age, museums and galleries proved to have a strong appeal to young people, particularly the 16-24 age group, and had a younger attendance than theatres and concerts. However, London had a younger age profile than the other three regions in the theatre and concert market, with the high student population reflected in the West End (including the national theatres), where over a third of the audience was between 16 and 24.

The size of the party in which people attended arts attractions was remarkably consistent in the three regional study areas. As one would expect, theatre and concert goers proved more gregarious than those visiting museums and galleries. Naturally, parties of two were the most common.

Another important characteristic of audiences, which is not obvious from the bare attendance figures, is the 'reach', a term which indicates the number of different individuals who attend in any given period rather than the number of tickets sold. The reach ignores how often people go.

Based on one or more attendances a year, the reach was almost identical in the three study regions, at just over 80 per cent for the top three social classes (ABC1) and 54 per cent for the rest (C2DE). But for two or more attendances in a year, Glasgow was prominent, with

Table 3.2   **Reach of the arts amongst ABC1s by region, 1985/86**

Percentages

	Glasgow	Merseyside	Ipswich
Percentages of ABC1s attending: (a)			
Museum or gallery	60	42	43
Art exhibition	22	26	24
Historic house	35	35	36
Play or musical	33	33	40
Classical concert	10	11	17
Ballet	11	8	5
Opera	2	4	4
Pop concert	14	..	14
Cinema	49	44	44
One or more of above	82	..	81
Twice or more	67	..	53

Source: page 29
(a) During 12 months previous to interview.

Table 3.3   **Reach of the arts amongst C2DEs by region, 1985/86**

Percentages

	Glasgow	Merseyside	Ipswich
Percentages of C2DEs attending: (a)			
Museum or gallery	30	31	24
Art exhibition	7	15	11
Historic house	12	20	21
Play or musical	11	20	20
Classical concert	4	2	4
Ballet	2	2	3
Opera	1	1	-
Pop concert	9	..	11
Cinema	26	27	26
One or more of above	54	..	54
Twice or more	31	..	27

Source: page 30
(a) During 12 months previous to interview.

41 per cent of all adults, 67 per cent of ABC1s and 31 per cent of C2DEs. In Britain as a whole, the arts reached two thirds of the population, based on one or more visits in a year.

Measured by type of event, the reach proved remarkably similar across the country. Some 31 to 39 per cent of the population visited museums, and a similar proportion the cinema. Plays and musicals were enjoyed by a quarter, concerts, ballet and opera by a tenth, and a similar proportion went to pop concerts.

Another way of looking at the picture is to find the frequency of attendance. Among local residents who attended at all, Glasgow scored highly within the three regions with an average of 3.9 attendances at museums and galleries and 4.4 at the opera. In Ipswich, where the choice is more restricted, the frequency of visits was lower. Of course, concerts, dance and opera have their ardent fans, so very active minorities can sometimes clock up a large proportion of total attendances. For example, an estimated 47,000 individuals bought the 249,000 tickets sold for the Royal Opera in 1982/83.

CHAPTER 4:
HOME ENTERTAINMENT
AND THE ARTS

Are TV and video killing live entertainment? In fact, attendance at arts events and attractions has recently risen despite the growth of electronic home-entertainment. What is more, there is a growing demand among audiences for higher quality and more choice.

There are still missing links in the statistical work which has been done so far. There is no really good indicator of the overall spending on the live arts. Nor do we know how far home entertainment affects live-performance ticket sales and prices - for example, the relationship between sales of CD players and concert tickets.

It is clear that while attendances at theatres and concerts have been increasing, so have the ticket yields. Chart 4.1 shows that the

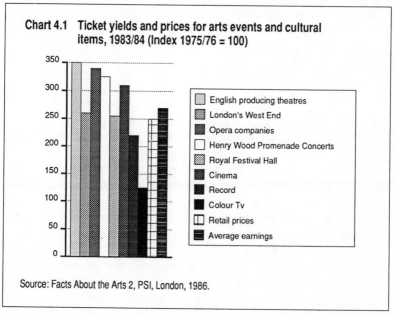

Chart 4.1 Ticket yields and prices for arts events and cultural items, 1983/84 (Index 1975/76 = 100)

English producing theatres
London's West End
Opera companies
Henry Wood Promenade Concerts
Royal Festival Hall
Cinema
Record
Colour Tv
Retail prices
Average earnings

Source: Facts About the Arts 2, PSI, London, 1986.

real cost of live entertainment has, up to 1983/84, risen, with spending on tickets increasing (with the exception, of the Royal Festival Hall).

There is a marked difference between movements in price for live events and those for records, which more than doubled in price, and colour TVs, which were only 26 per cent more expensive after eight years. Nevertheless, after some price resistance in the early 1980s, we know that attendance at live events has been growing. Presumably people are willing to pay more and go more often as they demand greater quality and wider choice.

Spending on arts events and attractions outside the home has as a result risen as a proportion of total spending on cultural and leisure activities. But spending on cultural and leisure goods - which includes newspapers, records, radios, TVs and musical instruments - remained over four fifths of the total. The new calculations of arts turnover later in the report are based on a more closely defined group which does not, for example, include newspapers.

Table 4.1　　Consumer spending on cultural goods and services: by main categories

Percentages

	1976	1984
Percentage of spending at current prices		
Recreational and cultural services		
(admissions and subscriptions)	16.2	18.0
Newspapers, books, magazines	25.2	26.0
Records and tapes	6.3	6.4
Photo processing and printing	2.9	3.2
Radios, TVs, instruments and other durables	48.6	46.4
Total	*100.0*	*100.0*

Source: Facts About the Arts 2, PSI, London, 1986.

TV and Videos win against Books and Newspapers

Looking at the volume of sales in Table 4.2, measured after adjusting for inflation, TV has grown enormously, particularly since 1980 when home video took off as a mass market. Records, tapes, books, newspapers and magazines did less well and indeed the record market was in crisis in the early 1980s, partly because of piracy and private copying. But with rising sales of pre-recorded cassettes and compact discs, growth began again in 1984.

Books were in graver trouble than records. Consumer spending on books, according to the Family Expenditure Survey, seems to have fallen by a fifth from 1980 to 1984 and there was a further sign of falling interest in reading at public libraries, where the number of

**Table 4.2   Consumer spending on culture and leisure
                 at 1980 prices**

Index: 1974 = 100

	1976	1980	1984
Cinema admissions	76	69	43
Other admissions (a)	118	139	125
Social subscriptions (b)	106	104	100
Books	95	105	84
Newspapers and magazines	91	90	84
Records and tapes	92	120	130
Photo processing and printing (c)	104	168	191
Radio, TV, musical instruments and other durables	112	147	264
TV and video hire charges, licence fees, repairs	119	136	168
Total	104	121	144

Source: Facts About the Arts 2, PSI, London, 1986.
(a) Includes admissions to arts events and attractions. Aso includes spectator sports.
(b) Includes spending on participatory sports.
(c) Photographic equipment included under 'other durables'.

books issued per head gently declined. The figures relate to a period before new enterprises and growing interest in high-street book retailing could take effect.

Not unexpectedly, the expansion of TV technology and services including video, cable, breakfast TV and the new Channel 4, persuaded people to spend more hours in front of the screen. The number of minutes spent viewing each day rose from 125 to 185 between 1977 and 1985, so that Britain was second only to Spain within Europe. Women and the elderly accounted for most of the rise, while the gap between social classes widened as the DEs increased their viewing much faster than the AB classes.

Nevertheless, the problems of the book trade and - to a lesser extent now - the cinema cannot obscure the fact that the market for the arts has been performing relatively well. The vital point is that attendance at arts events and attractions has not declined in recent years despite the rise of TV, videos and other home entertainment.

CHAPTER 5:
THE SIZE OF THE WIDER ARTS SECTOR

The arts attract £2.50 of every £100 of total fiscal expenditure in the UK. This represents the combined value of sales revenue and other income together with estimates of ancillary spending specifically attributable to the arts. It amounts to £10 billion. This is comparable with major industries such as vehicles and energy. The arts are more successful as exporters than manufacturing industry.

But to get to these figures it is necessary to look at the wider role of the arts. This includes the important spin-off from arts such as theatres and concerts - from tourist spending in hotels for example. It also takes in wider activities within the arts sector. The analysis in the next two chapters shows that the £10 billion is dominated by broadcasting, cultural products such as books and records, and by arts-related spending by tourists.

The report's estimate of the turnover of the arts is £10 billion in 1985 with a value-added of £4 billion. The estimate is specifically related to the narrow definition of performances and attractions, broadcasting and screen industries, books, records, arts and crafts and also spending on refreshments, hotels and other costs to the arts customer specifically attributable to events and attractions. The latter has a big impact, accounting for a quarter of arts turnover. (It is dealt with in more detail in the next chapter.) Historic buildings, libraries, architecture, fashion, advertising, graphic design, photography and education and training are excluded from the calculations. So are newspapers, magazines, musical instruments and equipment such as videos, radios and TV. Though all these businesses have a big arts content, they are not exclusively an arts preserve and their inclusion would be misleading.

Measured in this new way, the arts accounted for £2.50 in every £100 of total final expenditure by residents and foreigners within the UK. This puts them on a par with the vehicle market or sales of fuel and power. (Indeed with a looser definition, including all the industries listed as excluded, the figure would be more than doubled.)

In terms of value-added, the arts sector contributed 1.28 per cent of gross domestic product, roughly equivalent to motor vehicles and parts and somewhat smaller than agriculture, forestry and fishing.

Museums and Galleries

Museums and galleries (see Table 5.1 and Chart 5.1) had a turnover of £230 million in 1985 and a value-added of £141 million. This is far greater than the income figure in the previous chapter because it is based on all the money they receive and spend and not on the relatively small amount they receive from the public in admission charges.

National museums and galleries were supported mainly from central government funds, while local authorities paid for their own. Some museums made handsome earnings from teas and bookshops. Admission charges were made at only just over a third of the national museums, just over a quarter of the local authority ones, and 63 per cent of other museums, including the private sector independents. Public funds paid over half the income of the independents.

Table 5.1   Museums and galleries: income sources

Percentages

	Admissions/ sales (a)	Public funds	Private sources	Total
Mational museums and galleries (b)	7	93	..	100
Local authority museums (c)	5	91	5 (d)	100
Other museums and galleries (e)	37	53	9	100

Source: page 37
(a) Admission charges raised an estimated £1.2 million at NMGs, 2.4 million at local authority museums and £11 million at other museums.
(b) Office-of-Arts-and-Libraries-funded museums only: relates to 1983/84.
(c) England and Wales only, 1983/84.
(d) Includes 'other' income.
(e) Average of Glasgow, Merseyside and Ipswich, 1985/86.

Theatre

Turnover - the total of sales and other income - at 600 theatrical venues and in 350 independent companies in 1985 was estimated at £422 million, considerably higher than the box office figures used before, mainly because of subsidies (see Table 5.2). The scale varied from the Royal Opera House's £21 million (in 1983/84) to the 125

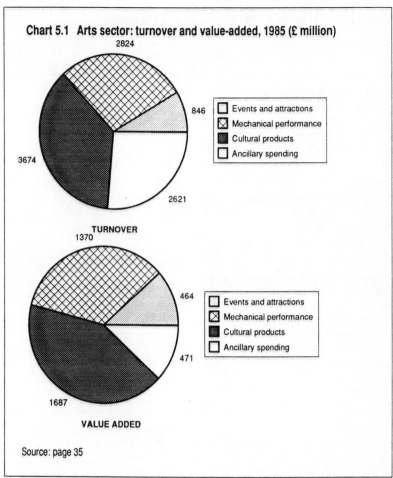

Chart 5.1   Arts sector: turnover and value-added, 1985 (£ million)

TURNOVER

- Events and attractions
- Mechanical performance
- Cultural products
- Ancillary spending

VALUE ADDED

- Events and attractions
- Mechanical performance
- Cultural products
- Ancillary spending

Source: page 35

companies in the Independent Theatre Council, which averaged £63,000 a year. Arts centres together with clubs, studios and lunch-time theatres provided half the venues, a fifth of the events and 8 per cent of the audiences, and their turnover was £53 million. But their artistic value was much greater than this suggests because of their role in small scale or development work and as a breeding ground for new talent.

The gap between box office receipts and outgoings has been filled by subsidies which have increased over the years, though there is now some evidence of a reversal as the subsidised companies have had to make a virtue out of stringency. Grants have had to go further and box office takings and other earnings have been pumped up.

**Table 5.2   Theatres, theatre companies and arts centres:
facilities, turnover and value-added, 1984/85**

	Number of facilities	Turnover (£ million)	Value-added (£ million)
Building-based companies			
National companies			
(drama, opera, dance) (a)	9	58	40
Producing theatres (b)	51	33	18
London's commercial West End	43	68 (c)	39
Sub-total	103	159	97
Venues			
Number-one receiving venues (d)	23	45	11
Local authority theatres	115	43	9
Independent theatres	51	25	8
Arts centres and small venues (e)	311	53	21
Sub-total	500	166	49
Theatre companies, producers, artists			
Main-scale opera, dance (f)	11	29	17
Small-scale opera, dance	20	2	1
Subsidised drama touring companies			
and projects	160	11	7
Other small drama companies	40	3	2
Commercial producers	120	25	21
Other (g)	..	28	23
Sub-total	351	97 (h)	71
Total	*925*	*422 (i)*	*217*

Source: page 38

(a) Royal Shakespeare Company and National Theatre £28 million 1984/85; Royal Opera House
and English National Opera £31 million 1983/84; the four companies operated nine auditoria.

(b) Turnover-includes 21 studio theatres attached to producing theatres.

(c) Box office only

(d) Including Glyndebourne Opera House.

(e) Includes 240 arts centres, several of which housed small producing companies.

(f) Scottish Opera, Welsh Opera, Opera North, Kent Opera, Glyndebourne Festival and Touring
Opera, Opera 80, London Contemporary Dance, London Festival Ballet, Scottish Ballet, Northern
Ballet, Ballet Rambert.

(g) Variety acts, circuses, dancers, overseas earnings from stage appearances by individuals.

(h) Less fee income received from venues, the figure was £21 million.

(i) The estimated fee income of £76 million paid by venues to companies is included twice in this
total, under venues and also under companies.

Subsidies grew in importance partly because of the contradiction of commercial theatres in the 1960s and 1970s. Outside London, local authorities are now the main providers of theatres. Private theatres and producers in the West End and elsewhere had a turnover of £170 million in 1985, just under half the total.

Table 5.3   Financing and the subsidised theatre

Percentage

	Box office and sales	Local authorities	Central government	Private sources
Percentage of income arising from different sources				
National drama companies	46	4	49	1
English producing theatres	48	21	29	2
Small companies	28	18	52	2
Dance companies	34	18	45	3
Opera companies	33	4	56	7
Local authority theatres and halls	53	47	-	-
Arts centres	37	43	17	3

Source: Facts About the Arts 2, PSI, London, 1986; Arts Centres in the UK, PSI, London, 1987.

Cooperation between the commercial and subsidised stage now includes the transfer of productions from the subsidised companies to the West End. More recently, public and private cash have tried out new and more chancy productions together, with the hope of an eventual commercial transfer. More private money has been going into theatre buildings but demand is rising for public money for the productions themselves. This interdependence is producing a more commercial outlook in the state-subsidised organisations, and it is now quite difficult to draw the boundary between the two sides of the business.

Nevertheless, subsidies remain important. State-subsidised theatre companies are expected on average to cover 30 to 50 per cent of their income from ticket and other commercial revenue: producing theatres are expected to reach the higher figure, opera, dance and small experimental drama companies, the lesser.

Music
Turnover of performers - including orchestras and soloists - together with the concert halls, was £194 million in 1985/86. Orchestra turnover was £40 million (17 principal orchestras, excluding 5 opera/ballet orchestras), while jazz, pop, folk and rock concerts were £19 million (which ignores the main source of income of pop musicians, the recording industry). Live performance of all kinds totalled £116 million while the venues in which they occurred took £73 million. Value added was £106 million, of which £88 million came from the performers. In addition to these live performance figures there is a very important part of the music industry which includes recording, publishing, instruments and equipment: together they have a turnover of £1.3 billion, of which £896 million comes from recording and royalties, (see Table 5.4).

Table 5.4   'Music industry' turnover, 1984/85

	£ million
Concerts	
Performers	116
Venues	73
Theatre music, live background music and other	25
Recording industry	896
Music publishing	88
Sound equipment	66
Musical instrument manufacture	57
Total	*1,321*

Source: page 42

Broadcasting, Film, Video and Cinema

The size of these businesses is important as a means of transmitting artistic ideas to the public, and an important source of earnings for performing and creative artists. It is accepted that much of the television and radio output has nothing to do with the arts. However, the figures for 1984/85 show that the BBC spent a total of £185 million on music and arts features, drama, popular music and variety shows, which represents one quarter of its expenditure; in comparison, the total independent broadcasters' spending on the arts for the same period was £219 million. Independent film and video production had an estimated turnover of £446 million in 1986: commercial videos claimed the largest part at £234 million. The exhibition of films in 1985 accounted for a turnover of £108 million (box office takings net of VAT).

Records, Books, Arts and Crafts

The £896 million turnover figure for records, mentioned above, included a healthy £391 million worth of exports and also the wholesale value of products sold in the UK, but it excluded retailing.

Publishing and printing of books produced income of £2,285 million in 1985 in 4,134 enterprises.

The organised fine art trade had sales of £859 million in 1986 according to a sample survey of trade associations for the report. Of this, £299 million was dealers' margin (gross income less purchase costs). The trade was heavily concentrated in London which accounted for a third of the membership of the four main trade organisations but for two thirds of the market. The dealers' margin of contemporary art dealers which did not belong to the four main trade bodies was £11 million.

An inquiry in 1982 put the dealers' margins on antiques, works of art and prints at £645 million, twice the margin in the organised trade in 1986, which suggests that sales for the whole sector were more than double those for members of the trade bodies.

Finally, assessing craft sales presents a problem because of conflicting definitions in Scotland and the rest of the country. The Scottish Development Agency put the turnover of 3,000 firms and crafts people at £39 million in 1984. The Crafts Council estimates of 7,000 full-timers in England and Wales combined with figures on turnover culled from the Ipswich case study suggest an £83 million total, giving a national total of £122 million turnover.

Earnings of Individual Performers and Creative Artists
This is not easy to calculate because of the transience of jobs among many creative people. A 1978 study showed that 54 per cent of actors' work was in the theatre, 19 per cent was on screen, radio and TV or other recording (which produced most of the money) and the rest in clubs or elsewhere. Musicians worked 12 per cent of the time in recordings or broadcasts, 14 per cent in concerts, 17 per cent in the theatre and 52 per cent in clubs, hotels and dance halls. Recording royalties were the main earners for pop musicians but for others the bread and butter was in live performance.

Combining this with data from a variety of sources in the industry, including the unions, it is possible to work out very rough estimates of earnings which totalled £153 million for actors and dancers and £339 million for musicians. (The latter was dominated by £281 million worth of recording fees and royalties, mainly for pop.)

Composers, song writers and similar creative artists earned £123 million of which recording rights, especially overseas, produced by far the largest amount. Figures for writers are more difficult to discover because they do not have access to the type of royalty collecting society which serves composers. But authors' royalties from the sale of books by UK publishers were £31 million in 1984 and a further £30 million was paid by broadcasting companies. Overseas earnings, grants, prizes and public lending rights took the total to about £75 million.

Crafts people and the enterprises they ran earned just over £50 million in England and Wales in 1986, calculated with earnings data including those obtained in the Ipswich regional survey. In Scotland, with a broader definition of crafts, workers earned £20 million in 1986.

Finally, painters and sculptors: new art purchases were put at £15 million in 1980. A more up-to-date estimate can be made by using the Glasgow study which put an average turnover of £110,000 on galleries dealing in new art. The estimated total of 200 contemporary galleries in Britain would on this basis sell about £22 million's worth, from which the artists would earn £13 million. The Ipswich survey also showed that artists received three fifths of their earnings from galleries, implying that nationally they could have earned a total of about £22 million in an art market worth at least £30 million. The Ipswich survey also showed that average earnings of full-time artists was a not over-generous £6,000 in 1986.

Overseas Earnings

The Arts are Fourth in the League Table of Top Invisible Earners.

Sales overseas contributed 34 per cent of the total sales for the arts compared with 27 per cent for manufacturing. The arts brought in £4 billion from abroad in 1984 (see Table 5.5). Of this total, four fifths was so called invisible earnings in the form of royalties, fees and spending by overseas tourists worth a total of £3.2 billion, placing the arts fourth in the invisibles league table after banks, travel and shipping, and ahead of civil aviation. The £900 million balance was made up from books, scores, instruments, records, tapes and craft items.

The largest single earner was £1.476 billion's worth of so-called cultural tourism, represented by the proportion of earnings from tourism traceable to arts performances and attractions in Britain, but excluding fares. The way this is calculated from surveys is explained later.

Table 5.5   Overseas earnings of the arts, 1984/85

£ million

	Goods	Invisible earnings	Total
Theatrical performances, films and TV material	33	426	459
Musical performance, composition, publishing, recorded and broadcast material	126	428	554
Publishing and the book trade	642	57	699
Art trade, visual arts and crafts	43	743	786
Miscellaneous transactions	12	28	40
Cultural tourism	-	1,476	1,476
Total	*856*	*3,158*	*4,014*

Source: page 47

The next largest earnings of £798 million came from the art trade, many of whose over-the-counter transactions in Britain involved payment from abroad. It makes sense to classify these as invisible earnings, because the art trade does not make the goods, it merely deals in them. There is some re-export from auction houses of goods which have been imported specifically to be auctioned. Craft exports at £43 million make a significant contribution.

The music business earned £554 million from overseas, a figure dominated by the £396 million earned in royalties on recordings. Live appearances overseas earned £10 million. Overseas earnings of the theatre, films and TV were £459 million, of which film and TV royalties and sales were by far the largest part. Earnings of theatre companies and other live appearance fees were £15 million. British stage artists were heavily restricted in North America, where they earned only £250,000 worth of fees compared with over £9 million in the rest of the world. But North America was the most important source of royalty payments to writers and creative teams for the overseas performances of British works valued at £20 million.

CHAPTER 6:
THE CUSTOMER EFFECT

A key to understanding the role of the arts in the economy is the way they generate growth in parallel consumer services. There is a huge spin off in spending by arts customers. This chapter uses new survey results to demonstrate how much arts customers spend on food, drink, shopping and other outgoings generated directly by their visits.

Concert, theatre and museum-goers do not spend only at the box office. The arts as a whole are a magnet for people who spend on food, drink, shopping, accommodation and souvenirs and who therefore boost the economy in many and varied ways. This 'customer effect', as we shall see, extends to subtler benefits such as vitalising city centres and improving their quality of life and general attractiveness, which contribute to regional development.

This section deals in detail with the customer effect using the results of special surveys undertaken for the reports. It concludes that people attending museums, galleries, theatres and concerts spent just over £4 billion in 1985/86.

Visitors often combine several purposes in one visit, so only a part of the spending and jobs should be counted as induced by the arts. The surveys indicate that purchases of £2.7 billion, 68 per cent of the total, can be ascribed specifically to the attraction of the arts which people were visiting. The rest of the £4 billion would have been spent whether or not the theatres, concerts, museums and galleries had existed.

The surveys, based on personal interviews, were undertaken by the British Market Research Bureau. Interviews at museums and galleries were conducted as people left; theatre and concert-goers were interviewed by telephone within three days, following an initial contact in the theatre or concert hall. There were 3,145 interviews in Glasgow, Merseyside and Ipswich and 807 interviews of overseas tourists in London, plus a small study of 255 London residents, day

visitors and British tourists. Detailed accounts of the methods used
and samples of the questionnaires are available in the full report and
in the three regional studies.

The survey data included a wide range of spending, from food
and drink to local shopping by visitors, to taxis and tourist accommodation. They excluded the cost of travel into the region and petrol, as
well as spending by those who gave shopping as their main reason
for being in the area. Residents were not asked about spending of a
routine local kind. The aim was to discover what spending had been
attracted into the regions *specifically by the arts*.

Who Spent What and Where

Not surprisingly, tourists spent more than day visitors, who in turn
spent more than residents. Theatre and concert-goers also spent more
than those at museums and galleries. Residents tended to spend more
in the locality during a museum trip than they would before or after
the theatre or a concert, even though the museum itself attracted less
of their money. Unsurprisingly, there are marked differences in
spending patterns between day and evening visits.

Tourists, spending about £28 a day, parted with surprisingly little
at the venues, spending more on shopping, food and drink elsewhere.
Average accommodation costs were little more than £10, the average
being brought down by the numbers staying free with friends or

Table 6.1   Spending by arts customers in three study regions:
average per visit or trip day, 1984/85

£

	In venue (tickets refreshments etc.)	Shopping nearby	Food, drink nearby	Travel in region	Other spending	Accommodation	Total
Residents							
Museums and galleries	1.49	2.40	1.34	1.02	2.88	-	8.85
Theatres and concerts	5.20	0.08	1.52	1.05	1.74	-	9.59
Day visitors							
Museums and galleries	2.53	3.56	2.56	1.84	2.75	-	13.24
Theatres and concerts	8.11	0.07	1.97	1.74	1.61	-	13.50
Tourists							
All	2.48	4.53	4.47	1.46	4.24	10.30	27.47

Source: page 66

relatives. In the Glasgow region, overall daily spending by overseas tourists excluding those visiting friends or relatives was almost £36, and even higher at almost £40 a day in Ipswich.

The London sample was smaller and less accurate, but some types of spending were clearly higher than elsewhere, especially on theatres and concerts (see Table 6.2). However, day visitors to museums and galleries actually spent less than in the three other study regions. The patterns of spending were remarkably similar throughout the country. This masked other differences, such as the larger number of London residents who spent something on food and drink. Day visitors to London, on the contrary, spent less on food and drink than those to the regions, perhaps because they ate snacks whereas elsewhere a meal was in order.

One surprise was that tourist outlays in London were not much larger than elsewhere. The average was reduced by the large number of long-stay European visitors, many of them young and staying with relatives.

Summer visitors from North America spent over £55 a day. In the autumn European short-stay visitors had the largest daily outlay of over £59. The latter is a very small part of the market, so given the amount spent this is obviously a market ripe for profitable expansion.

Table 6.2   **Spending by arts customers in London: average per visit or trip per day (a), 1984/85**

£

	In venue (tickets refreshments etc.)	Shopping nearby	Food, drink nearby	Travel in region	Other spending	Accommodation	Total
Residents							
Museums and galleries	1.68	4.55	1.17	1.05	4.55	-	13.00
Theatres and concerts	9.75	1.05	3.64	1.25	2.00	-	17.69
Day visitors							
Museums and galleries	1.97	1.57	1.21	2.30	4.65	-	11.70
Theatres and concerts	12.08	0.96	1.88	3.42	1.41	-	19.72
Tourists							
British (museums only)	1.79	5.89	1.52	3.44	9.13	11.52	33.29
Overseas	7.84	2.92	3.46 (b)	3.08	1.71	11.03	30.05

Source: Page 67
(a) Based on a very small sample of the figures with a wide margin of error.
(b) Some 62 per cent bought food and drink with an average spent of £5.58

31

In terms of spin-off spending, the survey data show that tourists have an overriding importance, accounting for two thirds of the total 'customer effect'.

This survey data is used area by area to estimate regional outlays and then national spending by combining it with what is known about total attendances. The details of the methods for the three regions, including allowances for multiple and cross-visits and for children under 16, are contained in the regional studies. Children were particularly important customers for museums and galleries - accounting for a quarter of Glasgow and a half of Ipswich visits - and are still significant at theatres and concerts. So allowances have also been made for them.

The results for the three study regions show the over-riding importance of tourists, who spent 60 to 70 per cent of the total of £165 million estimated as the 'customer effect' in Glasgow, Liverpool and Ipswich. This is more than the turnover of the arts organisations themselves.

The national picture shows that residents spent £628 million within their own regions and day visitors - less numerous but individually higher spending - laid out £288 million. But £3.1 billion (over three quarters of total spending) was by overseas tourists, of which London alone attracted £1.8 billion. (The figures are an approximation because they combine local survey data with countrywide figures. The London data are not as good as those for the regional studies. Cinemas and historic buildings are excluded, as are overseas tourist visits to London art trade and auction houses because available research resources could not stretch to them.)

How Much Spending is a Result of the Arts?

We need to know how much of the £4 billion is genuinely arts induced, rather than a side effect such as a visit to the opera during a business trip which would have occurred anyway. This was also explored in the surveys.

Home and overseas tourists were asked how important were museums, theatres and other cultural attractions in their decision to make the trip. If they said it was the sole reason, their visit was wholly attributed to the arts; if they said it was not a reason at all, all spending was excluded. Other answers were given a weighting as follows: very important, 90 per cent, fairly important, 70 per cent, small importance, 30 per cent. Residents were asked a slightly different question. What would they have done when planning their visit if they had known that the event they hoped to attend would be closed?

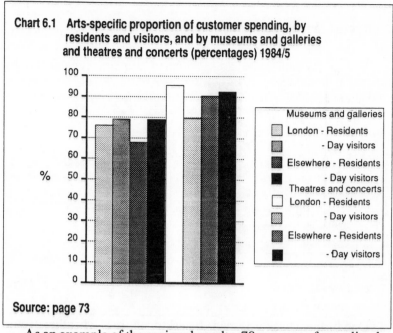

Chart 6.1   Arts-specific proportion of customer spending, by
residents and visitors, and by museums and galleries
and theatres and concerts (percentages) 1984/5

Source: page 73

As an example of the regional results, 78 per cent of spending by
'cultural tourists' in Glasgow was induced by the arts. For residents,
the same applied to 64 per cent of spending on museums and galleries
and 89 per cent of spending on theatres and concerts. The balance
would have been spent regardless.

As would be expected, museums and galleries are more popular
for casual visits than theatres and concerts which were more often the
main focus of an outing. The public was much less willing to accept
a substitute for a chosen theatre or concert programme than for a museum.

In the case of tourists, a smaller proportion of their spending was
directly attributable to the arts than in the case of residents and day
visitors, who are more likely to have come specifically and exclusively for the arts event. But the proportion of overseas tourists who
considered arts and culture a very important reason for coming to Britain was 43 per cent, while 7 per cent said it was the only reason.
Except for a high score on cultural interest from short stay European
visitors - another confirmation of the development potential among
this group of tourists - there was not much difference between visitors from various parts of the world. The proportion of spending by
overseas visitors directly related to the arts was at 68 per cent much
higher than for British tourists, at 57 per cent.

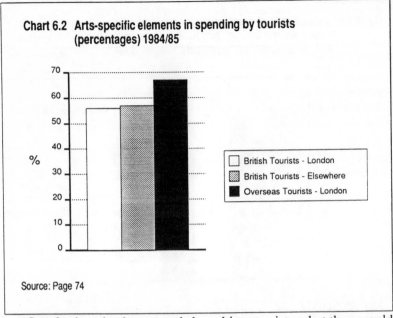

Chart 6.2 Arts-specific elements in spending by tourists (percentages) 1984/85

Source: Page 74

One further check was made by asking tourists what they would have done if the events they were supporting had not been available. Between 31 and 39 per cent would have delayed or cancelled their trips or gone elsewhere, with the top score from overseas tourists, confirming the strong attraction of the arts.

Finally by subtracting spending not specifically attributable to the pull of arts events and attractions from these results, the study arrived at a total of just over £2,758 billion for spending as a result of the arts, of which 74 per cent was accounted for by tourism, the rest by day visitors and residents (see Table 6.3).

The Arts have a considerable input into other Industries which the report has not attempted to quantify

No industry works in isolation. Arts turnover is only a part of the story because suppliers of food, drink, building maintenance and shipping services, specialist equipment and a whole host of other activities also make part or all of their living by dealing with theatres, museums and the rest. The 1986 British Theatre Directory listed several hundred specialist suppliers to the theatre alone.

The effects of arts spending go well beyond paying specialist suppliers. Payments to employees and suppliers - and subsequently to their employees and suppliers, and so on - are spent and respent as money changes hands. This generates additional income and employ-

Table 6.3   **Arts customer spending: total and arts specific proportion, 1984/85**

£ million

	Total spending	Arts-specific proportion
Residents		
Museums and galleries	288	202
Theatres and concerts	340	311
Day visitors		
Museums and Galleries	218	173
Theatres and concerts	70	57
Tourists		
British	950	539
Overseas	2,171	1,476
Total	*4,037*	*2,758*

Source: page 75

ment unrelated to the original activity. For example, theatres require electrical equipment. Electrical equipment manufacturers can afford to hire more staff, who use their wages to pay for housing and food, putting cash into quite different parts of the economy.

The borderline between fine art and design is hazy and there is no question that the arts are a great stimulus - as well as a source of ideas and people - to fashion, graphic design, printing, photography, advertising, architecture, interior design, textile design, animation etc. The arts even have an input into catering (hotel pianists), marketing (theatrical sales presentations), religion (church music) and defence (military bands, on which £36 million was spent in 1986)!

The arts also have a wider role in the percolation of ideas throughout the economy. This is suggested by the large proportion - 66 per cent - of the 190,000 people defined as in literary and artistic occupations who do not work in the arts industries. They are employed instead in retailing, catering, manufacturing and newspaper and magazine publishing. Even among the very specific group defined as actors, musicians, entertainers and stage managers, 1981 census results show that 23 per cent were still employed in other industries. However, such elements are not included in the above calculations.

CHAPTER 7:
GRANTS, SUBSIDIES AND TICKET SALES

The arts (events and attractions, mechanical performance and cultural products) raise 81 per cent of their income from sales of tickets, goods and services; 18 per cent from government and local authority grants; and only 1 per cent from private, including business, subsidy.

The financing pattern varies considerably within the arts as Table 7.1 shows. Examining one year, 1984-85, there were large sums of 'public' finance for the BBC in the form of £723 million worth of licence fees and a Foreign Office grant for the overseas service. There was very small government support for the film industry, which is also in the category 'broadcasting etc.'. But by far the greatest relative role for public finance is in museums and galleries, followed closely by theatres and concerts.

Table 7.1   Financing the Arts, 1984/85 (a)

£ million

	Sales	Public contributions (b)	Private contributions	Total (c)
Income				
Museums and galleries	23	189	18	230
Theatres and concerts	329	262	25	616
Mechanical performance	2,000	824 (d)	-	2,824
Cultural products	3,641	24 (e)	9	3,674
Total	*5,993*	*1,299*	*52*	*7,344*

Source: page 58
(a) Or nearest equivalent year for which figures were available.
(b) Excluding contribution to libraries, training, education and heritage.
(c) Revenue income only.
(d) Of which £723 million was from licence fees.
(e) Including £9 million spent on arts-related small businesses through Enterprise Allowances

Among theatres which produce their own work, and contract orchestras, a study has shown that the pattern has been changing, with a pronounced shift from public to private finance, mainly resulting from the growth of box office and other sales. Within public finance, local authority spending on the arts rose faster than central government contributions. Between 1981/82 and 1983/84, the most recent analysis of theatres and orchestras available, central government's contribution grew 21 per cent, sponsorship and donations 15 per cent, local authority grants 33 per cent and box office income and other trading (the largest single source) 34 per cent. These trends most probably are continuing.

Overall public spending on the arts has substantially increased over the last 20 years, with the growth fastest for local authorities. In 1983/84, excluding licence fees which are raised directly to support the BBC, the total was £450 million, of which £255 million was from central government. This includes Department of Education and Science spending on museums and £21 million of Department of Employment spending on arts-related programmes. Capital spending is harder to identify, but public sources provided at least £57 million in 1983/84.

Whereas local authorities have maintained museums and galleries for many years, spending on the performing arts is more recent. None of this is a statutory responsibility, so the effort varies around the country. Of the total, £67 million excluding debt charges was spent on museums and galleries in 1983/84 (more recent figures are not yet available), £75 million on theatres, halls and arts centres owned and operated by local authorities. A growing number of local authorities were directing increased support to independent arts organisations, which cost £35 million. Theatres and concerts, more than most, looked to all sources of finance they could get, including central government, local authorities, private donations and of course sales. Smaller organisations, the seedbeds for future growth, were the source of much experiment, which was one reason why they depended more heavily than other areas of the arts on public subsidy.

The arts have not escaped pressures for restraint on public expenditure in the changed political climate of the last few years. This has brought efforts to widen the sources of finance so that public expenditure has been complemented by growing private contributions, such as from commercial organisations, which either donate money or arrange promotional deals, or a mixture of both. The Association for Business Sponsorship of the Arts estimated sponsorship at £25 million in 1986.

In the three study regions, business sponsorship was of little importance to museums and galleries and private donations overall were more significant. In Scotland, the only region where there is a breakdown of figures, sponsorship went overwhelmingly to the opera and dance companies, the Scottish National Orchestra and festivals in 1983/84. But the evidence of the Business Sponsorship Incentive Scheme is that sponsorship has begun to reach less conventional areas of the arts.

The size of private contributions (donations and sponsorship) is not known but a total figure of £40 to £50 million for both kinds of support appears reasonable, helping to make the arts less dependent to a small but significant degree on government for their survival.

Links between Subsidies and the Commercial Arts
A good example of cross fertilisation is between broadcasting and the live arts, where film and television benefit from the skills of actors who polish their craft in subsidised companies. Without the commercial fee income it is difficult to see actors accepting the low pay of grant-aided companies, which also transfer their productions to the commercial circuits. There are similar relationships for many musicians. So public spending sustains the main arts organisations and produces trained people, tested products and ideas for the rest of the sector.

Rationale for Public Spending
The marketplace has nevertheless partly failed in the arts, as is clear from the fact that public help is needed. There has been a long academic debate about the rationale for public financing, and many explanations. For example, people may derive a general satisfaction from seeing cultural activity in the community at large, quite distinct from how much they participate themselves. Some may endorse arts spending in general but gain no more than a warm feeling from the enjoyment it gives to family and friends. There are also questions of local and national prestige, and the need to maintain an artistic legacy. In these circumstances, in which a service is supplied which people value for reasons other than their immediate enjoyment, public financing can be the most reasonable alternative.

At the end of the day, the simplest argument is that we have a glittering array of 2,000 museums and galleries, with changing displays and programmes of research and education, together with 1,000 venues and performing arts organisations providing over 100,000 concerts, plays, dance and opera performances a year - and all partly or mainly publicly funded.

Even so, the climate is ripe for encouraging those who do get most benefit from the arts to contribute more to their support. This trend is under way, with the growth in business sponsorship and higher returns from the box offices. Private individuals and organisations are taking a greater share of the burden of subsidy. On the other hand, if public funding is to continue, it is important to know whether the generalised benefits are agreed to exist by the population at large - both individuals and firms - which pays for them through taxation. This is discussed in later chapters.

CHAPTER 8:
THE ARTS AND THE CREATION OF JOBS

Are arts subsidies a better or more cost effective method of job creation than others which the Government is trying? First, we need to estimate the number of jobs there are in the arts, and that is not easy, especially as so many people with literary or artistic occupations are employed outside the core industries, and many of those who do work creatively in the performing arts are self-employed, part-time, or moonlight to supplement their irregular incomes.

To arrive at a current estimate of the number of jobs attributable to the arts, it is necessary to draw on figures from a variety of sources for a number of different years. We can make an estimate with some confidence 450,000 jobs in the arts sector, broadly defined. The Census figures for 1981 show 192,200 people employed in the arts on a definition which covers arts events, attractions, theatre, radio and television services and libraries. In the 192,200 is included 51,000 who worked as authors, composers and artists or who were employed by people in these categories. If the 99,000 in recording, books and arts and crafts are included, this gives an arts sector employing 291,000.

On top of these numbers, the arts generated an estimated 96,000 (1986 figures) in refreshments, travel and hotels, as explained in previous calculations. (A further 63,000 were in literary and artistic occupations in other industries, outside those covered by this report.)

Unfortunately, these national statistics are not good enough to detail the numbers working in each field of the arts. Other sources suggest that 19,000 work in museums and galleries. There are 8,000 in theatres which mount their own productions, 8 to 10,000 in theatrical venues of other kinds and 4,500 in opera and dance companies as part of an overall total for the theatre of 25 to 30,000.

Nobody knows the number of actors and dancers, though Actors' Equity had 32,000 members in 1984 of whom perhaps half were full-timers. There were about 4,000 full-time musicians, including 1,741 regular members of 22 principal orchestras, 750 session musicians and 1,250 engaged in theatres, dance bands and holiday camps. The tally excludes the 3,222 military bandsmen and thousands of semi-professional pop, jazz and rock musicians, some successful, others part-timers. Broadcasting employed 49,000, jobs in cinemas were 9,706 in 1984 and film production seems to have employed 18,000 or more.

Creative artists are the most difficult of all to count. The Performing Right Society collects on behalf of 13,000 UK composers and authors. The best guess for visual artists is 23,000 of which 6 to 8,000 might be full-timers. Nationally, there may be 35,000 craft workers.

The Growth of Jobs in the Arts

Jobs in the arts grew rapidly in the 1970s with an increase of 45 per cent in the number of actors, musicians and entertainers and 8 per cent in the number of authors, writers and journalists. The latest Department of Employment data show that this has continued and even accelerated, with 36,000 extra jobs created in the arts from 1981-86, almost half in museums, galleries and libraries. Fastest growth was probably in independent film and video production. Nearly 11,000 jobs were created in theatre, radio and television, a growth of 16 per cent. Such high rates of growth were a great achievement at a time when prospects in many industries were gloomy - and they were quality jobs, with few of them part-time. Men and women also shared equally in the growth, unlike the rest of the economy where the biggest increases have been in part-time and female jobs. The self-employed are not included in these figures but the number of self-employed is unlikely to have declined since 1981 when it was almost 61,000.

Assuming these trends have continued, it is safe to claim 486,000 jobs in the arts industries (including the arts-specific customer effect) and artistic and literary occupations in 1987. The number may well reach 550,000 by the end of the decade, confirming the arts' position among the major employers in the economy.

Now we move from the number of jobs we reckon are in the arts to the question raised at the start of this chapter, whether additional jobs stimulated by Government subsidy are value for money.

The best estimate of the cost to the public sector borrowing requirement of creating jobs and removing people from the unemployment count is £15,300 for current public spending, or £26,200 through public investment in infrastructure (Davies and Metcalf, Generating Jobs, Simon & Coates, 1985).

These figures are adjusted for tax paid by the newly employed and also for the effect of reducing the unemployment count (just over a quarter of new jobs go to those out of work). The report used the same procedure to calculate the net cost for arts jobs. The results compared very favourably with the national average figures, ranging from £1,066 to £1,361.

The extra cost of jobs in the arts was lower than for jobs arising from education and local government revenue spending (£10,400) and health (£10,700). The two sets of figures in the table are with and without the 'customer effect', which is the result of other spending by people attending arts events.

The same Davies and Metcalf study put the public spending cost of special measures for reducing unemployment, such as the Community Programme, at £4,920 overall and £2,200 net, after offsetting adjustments. The net figure for arts spending was lower in all three regions; the arts were a more cost-effective way of reducing the unemployment count than special unemployment measures.

Some government spending on special employment measures went to arts-related projects, often through the Community Programme, which provided temporary work for up to a year for long-term unemployed adults. In Glasgow and Merseyside £2.6 million was directed towards 760 posts of this kind. In Glasgow few of the jobs were for arts professionals but much of it was arts-related in one way or another, for example therapeutic use of arts and crafts and archive work in a museum.

There were some exceptions such as a sports and arts project in Glasgow in which most of the recruits had been trained in the arts. This had obviously uncovered an important need because numbers grew from 20 to 36 arts workers between 1985 and 1987. The Glasgow Council for Voluntary Services believed that demand for rehabilitation work based on the arts was so great that it would be possible to create hundreds of jobs for artists. However, there is no professional structure for this type of work and it gets little recognition from the social services.

Although Community Programme jobs last for only 12 months, according to one study a third of the people are in jobs seven months after leaving the schemes. Some of the Glasgow arts projects had significantly better results with as many as two thirds moving into jobs, while on Merseyside some projects were floated off into businesses.

The arts are exceptionally well suited to serving Community Programme aims, though the value of the projects to the arts is less clear cut. Museum and archive jobs have proved their worth, and others have found a valuable niche in applying the arts to social welfare. However, it would better to coordinate special employment measures with programmes serving the needs of established arts organisations, to help training and growth.

The Merseyside case study concluded that the new Maritime Museum and Tate Gallery would generate 825 jobs in the region with a cost to the public sector borrowing requirement of £386 per job. The new concert hall due for completion in Glasgow in 1990 threw up a cost for each person removed from the unemployment count of £1,518. These figures - which exclude capital cost - show the exceptional advantage of job generation through the arts because in both cases the average was less than for a Community Programme slot.

Any expansion of public borrowing is likely to raise fears that inflation will be stoked up. The case here is not for increasing public spending but for a switch of resources from spending on other types of special employment measures towards the arts which are a more cost effective area of job creation. The spending would be even less inflationary insofar as it could be targeted on areas of high unemployment. In any case the arts, especially theatre and music, have a chronic over-supply of labour, so there are unlikely to be inflationary wage settlements.

One fear is that winning extra audiences for new projects in the arts might be at the expense of existing attractions, displacing attendance rather than generating new activity. The evidence is that upwards of four fifths of attendance at new attractions in the arts represents real market gains.

CHAPTER 9:
HOW TO ASSESS NEW PLANS

Those who make decisions about investment in a particular region need to know the effect of the arts on job creation in that region (for some of the economic effects benefit suppliers etc. elsewhere).

One of the objectives of the study was to compare the economic impact of different arts projects within their own regions. To this end, the regional studies included economic impact analysis provided by DRV Research.

Comparing jobs, the total direct and indirect contribution of the arts sector in Glasgow was 14,735 or 2.25 per cent of total employment, a major part of the economy. On Merseyside it was 6,647 jobs, or 1.23 per cent, and in the Ipswich region it was 2,025 jobs, or 1.19 per cent.

Table 9.1   Economic impact of arts organisations, their customers and the cultural industries in Glasgow, Merseyside and Ipswich, 1984/85

	Spending (£ million)	Income (£ million)	Jobs (numbers)
Glasgow			
Arts organisations	25.5	11.4	2,620
Customer spending	66.6	13.9	4,185
Cultural industries	193.2	..	7,930
Total	*285.3*	..	*14,735*
Merseyside			
Arts organisations	14.0	6.4	1,698
Customer spending	60.3	7.9	3,405
Cultural industries	15.8	..	1,544
Total	*90.1*	..	*6,647*
Ipswich			
Arts organisations	4.4	1.7	610
Customer spending	13.9	2.7	781
Cultural industries	6.4	..	654
Total	*24.7*	..	*2,025*

Source: page 98

The arts organisations themselves generated income locally of £30 to £64 for every £100 of turnover, with museums and galleries on the higher side. The local contribution by individual performing companies varied greatly, particularly if they undertook national tours or hired many visiting artists. Glasgow proved to be more self-sufficient than the others.

The jobs produced by each £100,000 of spending by the arts organisations proved from the regional studies to range from 11 to 19, with museums and galleries having a higher impact than theatres or concerts. This apparently superior effect of investing in museums and galleries on both spending and jobs should be set against an earlier conclusion that museum and gallery visitors were less particular than theatre and concert-goers and more willing to accept a substitute. Theatre and concert audiences were certainly more dedicated.

The job numbers include part-time and seasonal ones, which was why Ipswich scored highest with 19 for each £100,000 of museum and gallery spending. Results also implied that suppliers to the arts organisations were concentrated in part-time, casual and low paid jobs.

Job creation impact can also be seen in the jobs produced by the 'customer effect'. This can be expressed as the number of jobs resulting from each £100,000 of spending by customers, which ranged from 4.6 to 6.7, much less than the effect of spending by the organisations themselves. This was because the businesses where customers spent their money paid proportionally more of the proceeds outside the region, to their own suppliers. However, as the arts customers spent much more than the organisations that they were visiting, their money did produce a lot more jobs in total. Tourists, as we have al-

Table 9.2   Impact of arts organisations in three regions: jobs generated per £100,000 turnover, 1984/85

Numbers

	Direct	Indirect	Induced	Total
Museums and galleries				
Glasgow	8.69	1.18	2.92	12.79
Merseyside	10.19	0.77	2.04	13.00
Ipswich	15.09	0.69	3.31	19.09
Theatres and concerts				
Glasgow	6.47	0.62	2.09	9.18
Merseyside	8.46	0.66	1.82	11.12
Ipswich	9.26	0.58	1.59	11.43

Source: page 100

Table 9.3   Extra jobs per 100,000 arising from additional arts trips
              in Glasgow and Ipswich, 1984/85

Numbers per 1,000

	Glasgow	Ipswich
Residents		
Museums and galleries	23	32
Theatres and concerts	35	10
Day visitors		
Museums and galleries	54	44
Theatres and concerts	31	24
Tourists	676	636

Source: page 104

ready seen, had the biggest impact, with 5.6 to 6.7 jobs per £100,000 spent. So fewer tourists than day visitors or locals are needed to produce the same number of jobs. In Glasgow, for example, it takes 287,000 theatre or concert visits by residents to provide 100 jobs, but only 57,000 separate days of tourist trips to have the same impact.

The result is that success in raising the number of tourist visits (averaging more than one day) by 50,000 would produce 338 more jobs in Glasgow and 318 in Ipswich - as many as a medium sized new factory. The analysis also tackled this from another angle, comparing the other jobs produced locally by the spending of the arts organisations and customers with each job in an arts organisation. The answers were 1.8 for Ipswich and a remarkable 2.7 in Glasgow and 2.8 in Merseyside.

Tourists were bigger spenders than other customers. For future development and investment they are clearly the best buy among an attractive range of options which makes the arts a powerful force in sustaining employment.

To look at the potential impact of a particular attraction, a special case study was undertaken of London temporary loan exhibitions. averaging the results for four separate locations. After deducting the effect of casual visits and concentrating only on spending specifically induced by the attractions themselves, it showed that each 100,000 visits injected £6 million into the London economy. Of the benefit, £2 million went to cafes and shops and £1.6 million to hotels. A blockbuster show attracting 500,000 visits injects £30 million into London. Such a scale of spending in Glasgow would sustain 1,650 jobs in the region.

CHAPTER 10:
TOURISM AND THE ARTS

Britain can offer immense variety to tourists: it has more culture than sun and major attractions such as Shakespeare country or the West End of London.

Before drawing conclusions about how to develop further the tourist markets, the chapter looks in detail at the relationship between the arts and tourism.

Museums and galleries depended heavily on tourists, especially in London, where they accounted for 44 per cent of visits, of which three quarters were from overseas tourists. Theatres and concerts were less attractive to tourists. Outside London the share was 5 to 10 per cent. However, in a special attraction such as the Aldeburgh Festival, the audience was 77 per cent visitors and 5 per cent from overseas. The Royal Shakespeare Theatre at Stratford-upon-Avon drew 60 per cent of its audience from more than 50 miles and 16 per cent from outside the UK. Tourists probably account for between half and one million attendances at festivals and special events.

It is hard to overemphasise the importance of tourists to the arts in London. They made up some 43 per cent of the market and 40 per cent of theatre and concert audiences. Overseas tourists accounted for 37 per cent of West End audiences in 1986, 10 percentage points

Table 10.1   Tourist and other attendance at arts events and attractions: in London and elsewhere, 1984/85

Millions of visits

	Museums and galleries		Theatres and concerts	
	London	Elsewhere	London	Elsewhere
Tourists				
British	3.5	7.3	0.9	2.4
Overseas	8.3	5.3	4.2	-
Sub-total	*11.7*	*12.6*	*5.1*	*2.4*
Day visitors	7.2	10.1	3.0	3.0
Residents	7.7	21.1	4.9	24.1
Total	*26.7*	*45.9*	*12.8*	*29.5*

Source: page 81

higher than four years earlier. At concerts they were only 8 per cent of the London audience, probably because music is more international so that London performances have a less distinctive quality.

These totals, nationally and in London, are probably an underestimate because they relate to museums, galleries, theatres and concerts, and exclude sightseeing - which often has a cultural side - and historic buildings.

There are many types of tourism, of course, from holidays and the conference trade to business, health and education journeys. The arts can be the main or a secondary reason for a journey. But are the arts important to tourism in general?

We have already seen that £3.1 billion, which is a quarter of the total £12.5 billion of tourist spending in Britain, is by people with an arts content in their trips. About 41 per cent of the £5.4 billion spent by overseas tourists, against only 13 per cent of the £7.1 billion spent by domestic tourists, falls into this category. The figures exclude fares to the region of the visit, and include all spending, not just that prompted by the arts, which as we saw previously was somewhat lower. In fact, the spending specifically induced by the arts was estimated at 16 per cent of the £12 billion tourism total, split between a remarkable 27 per cent for overseas tourists and 7 per cent for domestic tourists.

The survey of arts related tourism in London, which we first looked at earlier, gives other useful insights into foreign cultural tourism in Britain. North Americans were the largest group, followed by Europeans, with the rest of the world well behind.

Nearly a third gave sightseeing as their main reason for coming to Britain, followed by 17 per cent who cited visits to friends and relatives and 15 per cent who pointed to 'arts and cultural things'. Arts were much higher up people's rankings of their second reasons for visiting, only 4 points behind sightseeing at 29 per cent. Another interesting result of the survey was that North American tourists tended to be considerably older than the rest. It also showed that the average tourist stay in Britain was 20 days, with 14 of those in London.

Arts tourists spent much the same every day as other tourists but stayed longer and therefore spent more per trip - £613 compared with £373. North Americans figures prominently - 46 per cent of arts tourists yet only 26 per cent of all tourists. Another characteristic of arts tourists was a hard core of enthusiasts, such as those at Stratford-upon-Avon who averaged five theatre visits during their stay, twice the average. Americans went to the theatre more often than the rest.

The survey in London led to an estimate that 2.94 million tourists during the year took in the arts in one form or another, a third of the total tourist trips to London. On Merseyside, where well over half a million tourists and day visitors flowed into the museums as well as the seaside, the new class of cultural visitors was more likely to be from the ABC1 social groups, and to stay in hotels, than traditional visitors.

The Glasgow and Ipswich studies looked into cultural tourists in more detail and concluded that they were from a higher social class, older, from further afield, spending more and staying longer. The higher number of first time visitors showed that both areas had tapped new markets because of the influence of their arts, which was impressive because there had been little marketing from that angle. There was also some evidence that cultural tourism extended the season.

Glasgow provoked strongly favourable comments from tourists interviewed in the survey, which also showed that there was a great improvement in impressions of the City, comparing replies before and after a visit. This part of the survey was based on a series of statements about the City's buildings, museums, galleries, theatres and concerts. In fact museums and galleries made a much bigger impression than the live arts. Significantly, a third of all visitors and a quarter of first time visitors felt there was so much to do that they would have liked to stay longer, and over two thirds of cultural tourists said that they would probably return in the next three years. The Ipswich region was not quite as strongly appreciated by its visitors as Glasgow, but 80 per cent of first timers were likely to return there over the next three years.

There are obviously great opportunities to develop the relationship between arts and tourism for the benefit of both. But it is misleading to see arts tourism as uniform because people in the surveys who were in an area mainly to see the cultural attractions had different habits from those who fitted in the arts as an incidental extra.

The Glasgow and Ipswich studies concluded that it took special events to attract cultural tourists to theatres and concerts outside London. In spite of Glasgow's ability to present the widest array of regular dance, drama, opera and concerts in the UK outside London, these attracted few visitors from outside the West of Scotland. Regular arts seasons are difficult to sell to tourists unless they guarantee an exceptionally wide choice, as the West End does.

It is also worth bearing in mind the one-way traffic between museums and galleries on the one hand and theatres and concerts on the other. Visitors to the former are not very likely to go to theatres or concerts. But once a theatre or concert-goer is around, he or she is highly likely to go to a nearby museum or gallery.

The fact that arts tourism already has a high profile - four of the top six tourist attractions were museums in 1986 - does not mean that there is no scope for growth. On the contrary, the considerable achievements give a solid base on which to build, and despite international competition there is considerable potential for regions outside London to develop their arts tourism.

Arts tourism in the regions is a new and expanding market - 71 per cent were first time visitors in the case of Glasgow - with an up-market profile and high satisfaction levels, plus a willingness to consider repeat visits. The trend in Europe towards short breaks and greater sophistication among tourists points firmly towards selling the arts to attract visitors. Cultural tourists fill in the gap, in some areas, left by the decline of the traditional seaside holidays. Cultural attractions also help the conference trade sell its wares. Besides, major draws such as Shakespeare country or the West End of London can offer attractions ranging from crafts and museums to historic buildings and industrial monuments.

Tourism is clearly vital to the arts and vice versa. The importance of the links between arts and tourist earnings has not been fully recognised. A reassessment of the place of the arts in national tourism policy would be valuable.

Both current good practice and ideas for further development could be studied. A model is the six-year effort of the Society of West End Theatre to produce better understanding of the theatre's role in London's tourist industry. The London Tourist Board and Convention Bureau is likely to acknowledge the contribution of the arts in the tourism strategy for London now under development. Indeed, the travel trade is already selling theatre-breaks.

As examples of the kind of thinking which is required, the research showed that the major challenges facing Glasgow are to widen the appeal from the star Burrell Collection, exploit the strength of the performed arts, encourage repeat visits and collaborate with other parts of Scotland - for example in two-city packages with Edinburgh. Similarly for Suffolk, there is a need to widen the market and draw in more first time visitors, create two new flagships in the museums and the performing arts, and improve marketing in the county. The two case studies showed that the pay-off would be an extra 3,500 jobs in Glasgow and 890 in the Ipswich region.

Any project to expand arts tourism has to look carefully at the nature of the products which are to be marketed and how they can be identified locally. Initiatives must grow out of the region and not be grafted on. The travel trade, local authorities and arts organisations will need to work together. Cultural tourism should be linked to other aims such as improving the image of a region and developing the potential of city centres. Improvement of transport and accommodation are also important, as are specialist tourist services such as explanatory literature and signposting.

It is also important to have an organisation which can market and promote tourism in cooperation with the travel trade. The Greater Glasgow Tourist Board, funded by local authorities and the travel trade, fits the bill well. Suffolk at present has nothing between the four- county regional tourist board and the district councils. It is important among other things to plan arts schedules well ahead to fit in with travel trade timetables and to publish descriptive brochures. Equally, the arts community must be told how the travel trade works.

One of the most exciting challenges is to exploit the possibilities of cities and rural areas outside London, to spread the creation of wealth and ease pressure on the popular museums and galleries of the capital.

CHAPTER 11:
THE ARTS AND THE PUBLIC

Participation in the arts and belief in their public benefits is spread throughout British society. There was simply no support for the belief that the arts are of value only to a small minority. The view that public support for the arts should be continued at current levels was remarkable for its consistency across social classes and regions.

How are the arts perceived by the people who pay for them through taxation? Some interesting and sometimes surprising answers came from the regional reports which included a survey carried out by the British Market Research Bureau of a representative sample of 1,172 adults in the Glasgow, Merseyside and Ipswich areas.

The results contradict the popular belief that the arts interest only a small minority and show that the vast majority of people see a general community benefit from the arts. This included an improved image for their city or region, a feeling of local pride, a concern for future generations and - in the case of Glasgow - a belief in the general economic benefit of the arts to the region.

The survey of the three regions showed that almost two thirds of the adult population had attended an arts event or attraction in the previous 12 months and 32 to 41 per cent had attended twice or more. Museums and galleries were the most popular, reaching 31 to 39 per cent in the three areas; a third had been to the cinema; plays and musicals had attracted 17 per cent in Glasgow, 24 per cent on Merseyside and 28 per cent in Ipswich.

The higher social classes were more likely to have been involved in the arts more than once in the 12 month period. But even so those classified as C2, D and E showed significant interest across the board; between 11 and 20 per cent had been to one or more plays or musicals, and between 24 and 31 per cent had visited a museum or gallery (see Table 11.1).

Amateur involvement in the arts and crafts to some extent cut across social class. The proportion which actually participated in the

Table 11.1   Participation and attendance at arts events: by social class, 1984/85

Percentages

	ABC1	C2DE
Percentage of adult population		
Attending the following:		
Concert	13.5	4.0
Play or musical	20.0	15.5
Ballet/dance	8.0	2.0
Art exhibition	21.0	9.0
Engaged in the following:		
Choir/singing/playing musical instrument	16.5	7.5
Drama	3.0	1.5
Dance/dance classes	14.0	11.5
Painting/drawing	9.5	4.0

Source: page 124

arts and crafts ranged from 39 to 53 per cent in the three areas, and the fine arts - singing, music-making, drama, painting, drawing, sculpting or creative writing - involved between 21 and 29 per cent.

Higher class Glaswegians proved to be more active in choirs, playing musical instruments and amateur dramatics than their Suffolk counterparts; on the other hand, lower social groups from Suffolk were more active than Glaswegians in everything except playing a musical instrument. Glaswegians were more artistically energetic: more of them took part in a number of activities, though of course the opportunities were greater in a City than in a rural area.

Quite a few people were prepared to travel to arts events, 19 per cent of Ipswich area residents having attended something in London. Generally, Glasgow was more self-sufficient than the other areas in meeting the needs of its residents.

The survey proved that parental involvement in the arts was essential to stimulating children's interest. Not a single case cropped up of a child playing an instrument or singing in a choir or attending dancing classes outside school unless the parents were also involved.

What people thought about the importance of the arts

People were asked to rate in importance to themselves a list of amenities including parks, pubs, spectator sports and arts activities. Arts were important to 50 per cent on Merseyside, 42 per cent in Glasgow and 24 per cent in Ipswich (Ipswich citizens were influenced perhaps by having fewer local attractions). Museums and theatres were more popular than sports and night-life in Glasgow and Merseyside.

Table 11.2 Importance attatched to amenity factors by adult resident population of Glasgow, Merseyside and Ipswich regions, 1984/85

	Total population			ABC1			C2DE		
	Glas.	Mers.	Ips.	Glas.	Mers.	Ips.	Glas.	Mers.	Ips.
Percentage of adult population considering the following amenities important for enjoying living and working in region:									
Parks and public gardens	64	65	..	73	74	..	60	60	..
Access to countryside	54	67	67	72	74	75	46	65	61
Museums, theatres	42	50	24	59	61	32	35	45	19
Pubs, clubs, nightlife	40	45	41	39	31	44	41	52	40
Spectator sports	36	33	17	32	19	18	38	39	17
Fine old buildings (a)	33	53	51	45	61	63	27	50	44
Participation in sport	26	26	20	36	24	29	23	27	14
Lots of local activities to get involved in (b)	..	..	23	..	..	29	..	..	19

Source: page 127

(a) The question was about 'attractive towns and villages' for Ipswich region.

(b) Not asked in Glasgow and Merseyside.

But when asked to say how important the arts were for residents of their region in general - a significant difference - over 90 per cent replied 'very' or 'quite'. This cut across the social classes. The lowest score was from C2DEs in Ipswich. but it was still as high as 89 per cent.

Another question asking how important the arts were to the respondent produced consistent results across the regions, 70 per cent saying 'very' or 'quite'. It became clear that many people who did not go to museums, galleries, theatres or concerts still placed a high value on the existence of arts facilities. A social difference appeared. People in social classes C2DE placed less personal importance (63 per cent) on the arts than ABC1s (83 per cent).

Further questions testing responses to a list of approving and disapproving statements about the arts in Glasgow bore out this overall high regard for the arts. There was simply no support for the view that the arts were of value only to a small minority.

But did this pleasantly approving response mean that people were actually prepared to pay for the benefits from their taxes? Respondents in the three areas were told how much public money went into the arts locally every year (a wide range from £4 per resident including children in Ipswich to £10 in Glasgow). They were asked 'Do you think this amount should be increased, remain the same, be decreased or be stopped altogether?'

Table 11.3 Valuation and use of the arts by adult resident population of Glasgow, Merseyside and Ipswich regions

	Glasgow	Merseyside	Ipswich	ABC1	C2DE
Percentage of adult population considering the arts important:					
For the residents of a region	95	91	93	95 (a)	92 (a)
For themselves personally	71	51 (b)	69	83 (c)	63 (c)
Percentage attending an event of attraction (d)					
At least once	62	..	65	81 (c)	54 (c)
At least twice	41	32	37	60 (c)	29 (c)

Source: page 128
(a) Average of Glasgow, Merseyside and Ipswich.
(b) Percentage considering arts important for enjoying living and working in Merseyside.
(c) Average of Glasgow and Ipswich.
(d) In 12 months previous to the interview.

The strongest view was that support should be maintained, and most of those asked thought, irrespective of social class, that the existing level of funding (however different in each region) was acceptable. This disposition suggests that a higher figure might also be acceptable if public understanding of the benefits could be increased - the more so since a large minority already thought the amount spent should be increased. Few wanted any reductions.

A supplementary question in Glasgow and Ipswich asked those who wanted higher spending on the arts whether they would willingly pay for it from tax, and around two thirds said yes. Merseysiders were asked to name a figure. A quarter set it as high as £7 to £10 per head per annum (against actual spending which they were told was £4.45). The survey did not actually ask how willing people were to make donations or pay admission charges, but the warm public response does suggest that they may be readier than usually recognised to dip into their pockets.

CHAPTER 12:
THE ARTS AND URBAN RENEWAL

A vibrant arts life can have an important impact on the fabric as well as the heart of a city.

The arts are a great draw to people at home and abroad and a powerful inducement to spending of many kinds. They are also a potent force for improving the environment and encouraging regional and urban development. Arts projects can build confidence among an area's politicians, financiers and the public; enhance prestige, create local jobs, serve the local population and entice people to spend money in the locality. They have a strong pull on the more prosperous and in the right circumstances the effects of arts developments can spill over into surrounding areas. By bringing life to city centres, the arts also make them safer places.

Artists were involved at the beginning of the rise of Glasgow's Merchant City: they started group studios in derelict buildings, so successfully that their presence spawned more studios, workshops and designer shops of an attractive and lively type - to the point that rising rents now threaten further developments of the same sort. Bookshops, architects, advertising agencies, graphic designers and other office trades naturally followed, and though rising rents are a problem, they can be turned to the artists' advantage by persuading developers to include space for them in new projects. There is a good case for a study of how arts organisations can best take advantage of finance and property development.

In contrast, Liverpool's Albert Dock benefited from two major new facilities, a new Maritime Museum and the Tate Gallery, Liverpool, recently opened. This development is a public and private partnership involving the largest collection of Grade 1 listed buildings in Britain. It puts the exploitation of Merseyside's cultural heritage at the centre of a redevelopment strategy which is already building confidence in the future prospects for the region.

In Ipswich, a European Visual Arts Centre is proposed for the working Wet Dock which has under-used historic commercial buildings. It should also be a catalyst for other development in the area.

The three regional studies give a graphic illustration of the magnetic effect of the arts which pulls residents, visitors and tourists into the vicinity of theatres, concert halls and museums. Over 90 per cent of regional residents and day-visitors gave the theatre or concert performances they were attending as their main reason for coming to the area, and a similar answer was given by 67 per cent of tourists in the Ipswich region, where Aldeburgh is a strong influence. There was a marked but less dramatic pull from museums and galleries, though casual trade was more significant for these.

Street entertainers and musicians have their supporters and increase the attraction of an area. The evidence from the Albert Dock on Merseyside was that this did little to increase the flow of customers, which was more effectively accomplished by concentrating resources on major arts facilities and attractions and special events. This is consistent with the research, which showed that visitors and tourists come because they want to see specific things.

Perhaps the best example of the way the arts can re-animate city life is the Glasgow Citizens' Theatre, which stood out as the sole public building in a large part of the Gorbals, then being cleared. The theatre audience remained loyal and the Citizens', the last trace of city life in an urban wilderness, became a symbol of continuity with the Gorbals' past, and the nucleus around which a new society could form. The quarter is now being successfully resettled and its spirit has endured in the theatre and its audience.

CHAPTER 13:
ARTS AND BUSINESS

Investment in the arts and other amenities is becoming part of a new spirit of competition to create the right environment for business investment and to attract talented people to work in a region or a city's industries. This is not just a competition among Britain's cities and regions. It is becoming European and worldwide as nations chase investment and high calibre people.

A strong 'cultural infrastructure' is certainly a business asset for a region. This was proved by the regional studies which included interviews with top executives in 63 companies and organisations. They were asked in structured one hour interviews about their family involvement in the arts and about how far they saw a role for cultural attractions in bringing new businesses and good executive recruits to the region. The survey also examined the scale of business sponsorship of the arts. These managing director and partner level interviews were supplemented by a survey of middle managers. This chapter is about the results.

Glasgow
It was hard to find a leading businessman in Glasgow who did not have an involvement in the arts, and for most of them it was extensive. Nine of the interviewees had between them served on the boards of 15 different arts organisations. Several companies had bought or commissioned paintings and all used arts in one form or another to entertain clients and employees, including sponsored nights out at the opera and business entertainment using facilities at the Burrell Collection. The links between business and the arts in Glasgow were therefore unusually strong and deep rooted in the City's history.

The recent 'Glasgow's miles better' campaign and Glasgow Action - a group of businessmen and politicians - have strengthened the business links with the arts which had long been a focus of civic and national pride. The campaign, conceived by the business community and the Lord Provost, began by improving the morale of Glaswegians, and there is evidence that it has also improved media coverage and the image of the City elsewhere. A vital part of the improvement was a better perception of Glasgow's cultural reputation, which elsewhere in Britain was hardly known.

Everyone interviewed thought that the arts had played a major role in improving Glasgow's image, and that the then forthcoming Garden Festival and the designation of Glasgow as European City of Culture 1990 would be good for business and would increase tourism. Most thought that once people had been to Glasgow and found the reality, rather than the grimy image, there would be a lasting improvement in the City's reputation. They also thought it would convince outsiders of the benefits of working there and even lead to relocation of businesses in the City. There was widespread belief that the City would profit from the European City of Culture designation. Glasgow's commitment to the arts was deeper than Edinburgh's, whose arts festival was regarded as an annual 'flash in the pan'.

Ipswich

The arts were less important to Ipswich businessmen, though this may be changing as new companies move into the region and others expand. Services are becoming a more important feature of the local economy. There are more executives moving into the area and they are often the ones most critical of the night life, especially if they have come from London. Some local business leaders are ambitious to put Ipswich on the map as a prestige business address.

All those interviewed had personal experience of the arts - theatre and historic buildings were most often mentioned - but few had extensive contact. Business entertaining was more likely to be in a country restaurant than at the theatre or a concert. Many of the companies moving into the area had a branch mentality, as parts of national groups, so that the plusher forms of entertaining were more often done by head office in London, which was near enough for local executives to visit frequently. However, indigenous firms took a different view. Growing sponsorship came from relatively small firms as demand rose for better facilities so that the arts would meet the increasingly sophisticated needs of an expanding region. Unlike Glasgow and Merseyside, Ipswich started from a strong base; it had no grimy smokestack heritage to counteract.

Merseyside

The arts were one of the slender threads holding together Merseyside as a viable region, according to many of the businessmen interviewed in 1986, especially those in the larger companies. They warned that at a difficult time in Merseyside's economic history any decline in the level of arts could break Liverpool's fragile hold on its status as a sophisticated city, which was vital to its economic future. (The Royal Liverpool Philharmonic seemed threatened at the time.) One executive said 'the arts define the soul of Merseyside and its sense of place'.

Although many executives and their families were very involved in the arts and the amenity importance was widely recognised, the arts had not yet fully suffused the business culture of Merseyside in the way they had clearly done in Glasgow. There was also room for improvement in understanding between the arts and parts of the business community, in spite of successes such as an industrial subscription scheme in which companies buy tickets at a discount for their employees, and the major financial contribution to the arts of the John Moores Foundation, funded from a successful local business. Sponsorship was developing but not on the Glasgow scale, and some companies, especially the smaller ones, were sceptical about the benefits, regarding their clients and Merseysiders in general as philistines. However, the Council for Business and the Arts in Merseyside has been set up by businessmen to educate and inform on sponsorship.

Another contrast with Glasgow is what one executive called the 'lack of a practical blueprint for the future of Merseyside which will enable people to be positive, optimistic and to have a vision'. But the £100 million development of the Albert Dock was regarded, like the Burrell Collection in Glasgow, as a symbol of future improvement, with its Maritime Museum, Tate Gallery and TV studios. Half of the money was to come from public and half from private sources, though 90 per cent of up-front spending had so far (in 1986) been public. What is missing, again a difference from Glasgow, is an economic blueprint for the whole city centre beyond the waterfront developments. Executives appeared to want an imaginative and complete rethink of the packaging of Merseyside to attract service industries, high technology and tourism, with amenities and cultural attractions as a central feature.

How the Arts Influence the Location of Industry

Companies prefer not to move unless they have to, but when they do, decision-makers weigh up the quality of life alongside cost, convenience and financial incentives. The arts have an influence, as part of the quality of life.

In Glasgow, nobody could say for certain why firms chose the area but those responsible for selling the idea to business believed that without a strong cultural infrastructure their task would be more difficult. They said that the arts reputation of Glasgow has attracted a number of inquiries, especially from US companies which regarded cultural assets as a 'real bonus'. The arts were strongly featured in selling Glasgow to journalists, politicians and businessmen. Hard business facts, as well as grants and other incentives, were the prime concern, but companies took thriving culture as evidence of a dynamic self-confident community.

Among senior executives - some of whom were attracted to Glasgow because they were Glaswegians, making analysis of the role of arts difficult - the job offered was usually the key factor. The arts helped keep people and offered a pleasing lifestyle to those already committed to the City for other reasons, though they could swing the balance for the undecided.

Unlike Glasgow, Ipswich had no grants to offer, so business facts were the key consideration - either the local market, access to raw materials or good transport. But employers are increasingly concerned about better amenities for themselves as well as their staff and there was a body of opinion that 'more to do in the evening' would encourage industry into the region. While many managers did not think the arts important in recruiting senior staff, some (such as a major telecommunications organisation employing highly educated people) took the opposite view. Once having moved, as one employer said, 'we could not keep staff here without the arts'.

Because of its decline, Merseyside was not a good place to test the effects of culture in influencing firms to move to the region: too few firms had recently done so. But executives said that personal tastes such as an interest in sailing or the arts influenced the highest levels of management when deciding on a move, and the arts were one of the crucial factors in retaining managers and technologists already there.

The Middle Managers' Views
Willingness or unwillingness to move involves a complex of motives, some personal. Some middle managers were hesitant about moving to Glasgow or Ipswich, citing schooling or house prices; occasionally some took redundancy. Glasgow's lifestyle was not as important in selling the idea of moving as promotion and an appeal, in the case of Scottish expatriates, to return to their roots. But once they had moved, enjoyment set in and few wanted to return South. So while

in both Ipswich and Glasgow relocation had worked, the process of actually carrying it out was difficult. Quality of life arguments were not particularly influential in persuading less senior grades, the bulk of the staff, to move.

While culture is a positive influence on employment, it is better at holding people than pulling them to an area. A survey of younger and more mobile middle managers, in which 238 questionnaires were completed, provided an insight into attitudes in the three regions. Interests proved similar to those of the local population, but the middle managers were much heavier users of arts facilities, especially on Merseyside. Though 74 per cent considered museums, theatres, concerts and other cultural facilities important in choosing where to live and work, they rated below environment, housing and transport.

Further questions more specifically about leisure put culture an equal second (with siting of fine old buildings) to access to pleasant countryside. The middle managers were also keener than most on increasing subsidy for the arts, even through higher taxes.

Cross-checking managers' opinions of the other regions' cultural facilities and their views on moving there themselves produced some interesting confirmations (see Table 13.1). Positive views of culture in Glasgow and on Merseyside, seen from afar, had not overcome the cities' more general bad images.

Nearly half of Glasgow managers were happy to contemplate living in Suffolk with its attractive towns and villages and pleasant countryside, in spite of low scores for their impressions of its cultural facilities. Those who were happy to move to Glasgow or Merseyside were no more impressed by the two regions' museums and theatres than the rest of the sample, which did not like the idea

Table 13.1   Middle managers' reasons for enjoying and working in three regions, 1984/85

		Respondents in		Percentages All
	Glasgow	Merseyside	Ipswich	respondents
Percentage regarding as important:				
Access to pleasant countryside	93	91	94	93
Museums, theatres, concerts and other cultural facilities	79	68	60	69
Parks and public gardens	74	73	40	62
Fine old buildings	60	51	96	69
Participation in sporting activities	51	56	56	54
Pubs, clubs and nightlife	32	37	80	50
Spectator sports	26	39	10	22

Source: page 140

of moving. All this leads to the finding that while culture helps people to stay it does not persuade them to want to move. If they have to move, then the arts are one factor in reconciling them to the prospect, especially after their arrival.

The Surveys were used to Assess the Extent of Business Sponsorship of the Arts

The scale of sponsorship is one test of the value of arts to business. The surveys estimated it at £540,000 in Glasgow - which had more success in raising funds outside the region because of its prestige orchestra, opera and ballet companies - £183,000 on Merseyside and £72,000 in Ipswich (see Table 13.2).

Only a minority of companies were interested, though half of the executives interviewed, mainly in middle and large scale companies, had been involved. The sums ranged from £50,000 down to a single corporate membership of the National Trust. Ipswich sponsorships were small because so many of the companies were branches; some Ipswich executives were anxious for the sake of their own operations to turn the area into a prestige business address. Some local companies saw no direct benefit in sponsoring the arts, especially when their products were not aimed at the nearby market, a view expressed in a lower key in Glasgow and on Merseyside.

Other companies, especially in Glasgow, took a wider view of the business benefits to be gained for the region, in improved status, making it a better address. There were also direct business benefits, such as being a good employer by offering tickets to staff or using the arts to entertain business associates. A number of major companies wanted to promote a product or brand name but this was unusual. There is scope for expanding the modest contribution of smaller companies and ending the 'branch mentality' of some of the larger ones.

Arts and crafts people - and firms - had a slightly different view when surveyed in Suffolk. They claimed an indefinable way of life

Table 13.2   Business sponsorship of the arts in Glasgow, Merseyside and Ipswich, 1984/85

	Number of sponsorships	Total sponsorship (£)	Sponsorship from local firms (£)	Average sponsorship (£)
Glasgow	158	540,000	144,000	3,165
Merseyside	65	183,000	113,183	2,815
Ipswich	61	72,000	35,000	1,180

Source: page 142

as the main advantage of the area even though local residents were not the main customers. 75 per cent of artists cited the beauty of the area itself as an inspiration to their work, but only 41 per cent of crafts people. But both arts and crafts people were dissatisfied at critical neglect, which they put down to being too far away from London.

International Competition
Longer term investment in the arts and other amenities are becoming part of a new spirit of competition among European and world cities which are chasing growth industries and high calibre people. Studies have shown that modern industries often do not need specific locations as the old industries did, because telecommunications and transport have improved. Companies can choose to be where life is congenial, away from congestion, now that large central headquarters are less necessary. Working the other way, markets and specialisms also seem to be concentrating in fewer places because some businesses feel the need to be near centres of political and financial influence, and to sources of creative energy. Both developments make amenity more not less important, because they call for greater efforts to make a shrinking number of growth locations more desirable places in which to live.

Furthermore, European Community limits on financial incentives to businesses to move may make museums, theatres, concert halls and other amenities a useful way to counteract the lure of more central parts of the Continent and the warm climates of Southern Europe. Competition among medium-sized towns in the South East is already fierce and amenity has become a hard business fact there, to be considered alongside other locational factors.

Internationally, New York, Paris and London compete for footloose headquarters and high-powered individuals in search of sources of influence and creativity. The French government is investing to make Paris a greater cultural centre, lavishly adorned with new museums, a new opera house and other grand projects, and host to the world's greatest artists and performers. London is fighting back with improved communications and expanded office space, but makes less of its arts and culture than do the French. Even so, as the favourite destination of travelling businessmen, London seems well placed in the international competition.

The arts bring a competitive edge to a city, a region and a country as a source of creativity and a magnet for footloose executives and their businesses.

CHAPTER 14:
THE TASK OF FULFILLING
THE ECONOMIC
POTENTIAL OF THE ARTS

The report has shown the large and growing importance of the arts to the economy and the multitude of possibilities for development. At this point we draw some of the strands together. A critical aspect of the development of the arts is that it cannot be achieved by any one group in isolation. The groups involved include central government, development corporations, task forces, local authorities, arts organisations, public bodies in the arts and tourism and of course private business. An understanding of the role of the arts in tourism, regional development, inner city regeneration and rural development is central to appreciating the economic potential of the arts.

Central government has an opportunity to recreate a more favourable national climate for the economic expansion of the arts by its co-ordinating role and by the use of resources. At the local level, development corporations, task forces and local authorities are key organisations, and they too need to improve co-ordination both among themselves and with regional arts associations, area museum councils and tourism bodies. The partnership will extend to the private sector and to the local business community. Some agencies, especially at regional and local level, will wish to devise new strategies to fulfil the economic potential of the arts, while others will want to relate the arts to existing tourism or economic strategies.

The process will be made easier because the arts are expanding after a lull in the early 1980s. There is a growing demand for higher quality and choice which includes ease of travel, parking, and comfort in its broadest sense, qualities which should be carefully monitored. Important parts of the arts are in a leisure market which according to one forecast will expand by over a quarter by 1992.

The cultural industries have also expanded, especially television and video; while film, video and broadcasting are entering a period of rapid change in a market whose growth owes a lot to the rising demand for quality and choice. Independent film and video producers, for example, will benefit from the increasing use of their programmes by the statutory broadcasting organisations, in line with the recommendations of the Peacock report.

One risk is that London - rather than the regions - becomes even more dominant as the grip of the BBC and ITV is relaxed and big independent media conglomerates may grow to rival the existing organisations. This could be a major challenge for London and an opportunity for promoting several other British centres for the screen industries such as Glasgow and Cardiff.

With 23 per cent extra jobs in the arts between 1981 and 1986, many of good quality, there is scope for further increase in employment, though broadcasting and film employment may grow more slowly than output because there is considerable room for higher productivity within existing manning arrangements.

The growth in this sector since the early 1980s has not been created by increased central government funds, nor has it come from market forces alone, though higher box office receipts have been the great driving force. Local authorities have made a major contribution, while private sources have provided more funds and an important symbolic role. Productivity appears to be rising in arts organisations, too, and new technology has boosted growth in the reshaping of the home entertainment industry, computerised box offices and the management of museum collections.

In the background, rising incomes are playing a significant role. Ticket prices have risen faster still, interest in the arts is also closely related to the spread of education, especially further and higher education which are expected to increase. A better educated population with more leisure is bound to enlarge the market for the arts.

The Opportunities

1. Arts and tourism

• The relationship between tourism and the arts is reciprocal and the potential for further development considerable, as arts tourism is a relatively new phenomenon. Arts tourism can help to iron out seasonal variations. Saturation of the tourist market has been a real fear, but the shift towards short breaks, sophisticated tastes and activity holidays reinforces expansion of the tourist market.

- Strategies for arts tourism could be developed, further making use, for example, of the body of experience developing in London.
- Some reassessment of the arts in national tourism policy is needed, to recognise their place and to identify good practice, and new developments.
- There is a particular challenge in exploiting cultural assets in the great cities other than London and rural locations.
- Tourism creates a demand for unqualified labour, but skills in the tourism industry are rising and an expansion of the arts as a main tourist attraction will call for more skilled personnel.
- New arts initiatives for tourism should grow out of existing arts organisations and the needs of the local community.
- Effective co-ordination between local authorities, the travel trade and tourist and arts bodies will be essential. The same applies to means of marketing and promoting arts tourism initiatives.
- Broader tourism objectives should also be brought into play, including improved transport and communications, and other tourist services.
- Arts organisations will have to support efforts to encourage investment in tourism.

2. *Urban development and renewal*

- The arts are a magnet drawing people who spend money, and directly and indirectly creating jobs. The arts build confidence in a locality, enhance prestige, and service the needs of the local population. As Glasgow demonstrated very clearly, arts organisations can be a catalyst for development, and can create opportunities by raising the value of a neighbourhood.
- The arts can help find uses for refurbished property, which brings a planning gain that in turn makes co-financing arrangements attractive.
- A study is needed of the opportunities for arts organisations provided by property financiers and developers who could include studio, rehearsal and performing space in projects, and incorporate visual art elements for the public.
- A comprehensive approach is required to realising the value of the arts as a business asset through public and private partnerships in which business can take the lead. As Glasgow shows most strongly, the arts offset decline, promote regeneration, improve a city's image and help to keep executives in the region. There is a new spirit of competition among the world's cities, which

compete for expansion projects and jobs through investment in amenities. Additionally, the arts introduce a potent source of creativity into the life of a region, with spin-off into other productive activity.

- Marketing also needs advice and assistance, especially as many small firms in crafts or design are the seedbed for future growth.
- As the creative process involves high risk - in recognition of this public funds are pumped into the film industry, for example - special consideration should be given to the creative industries generally. Soft loan arrangements could be extended.

3. *Rural areas*

- Ipswich was the chosen area for a rural case study. It showed that the arts, surprisingly for a dispersed population, reached as many people as in other regions, and the reach was even higher for the theatre.
- There was some local criticism of the choice available. Live arts were mainly touring performances and little creative activity was originated in the region - only four of 13 organisations mounted their own productions.
- The Ipswich region's small venues, such as the Quay Theatre, Sudbury, attracted a much wider social mix than most metropolitan venues.
- Arts and crafts and antiques were a larger part of the arts sector in Ipswich than in the other two regions studied. The Ipswich report suggested as means of realising the economic potential of the region:

  building up the arts and crafts;
  expanding arts related tourism, especially cultural short breaks;
  providing a large receiving theatre for touring productions;
  developing a new museum to act as a flagship for museum and heritage tourism;
  expanding the creative base of the live arts by establishing a dance company and a chamber orchestra;
  establishing regular Suffolk Seasons of concerts, drama and dance in selected small towns and villages.

4. *Regional variations*

- The regional reports showed big differences between the three regions surveyed outside London, with Glasgow by far the biggest centre for the arts. There are also regional imbalances in employment, with over a third of the arts related jobs in Greater London, where more than half the radio, TV and theatre jobs were concentrated.

- The Commons Select Committee on Education, Science and Arts said in 1982 'We wish to ensure that people have a more equal opportunity to participate in the arts than at present so that the arts will flourish as widely as possible'. The aim might also be to share more equally the economic benefits of the arts, which in the tourism context would disperse visitors more widely across the country, an important objective of the tourism authorities.

5. *Jobs*

- Extra jobs will arise in the arts from the expansion of the independent sector as well as from growth in the subsidised. The initiatives must lie with the sector itself, but public agencies can help independent organisations. Where the sector consists of small firms, there can be benefit in drawing it together into a single voice for promotional or other purposes. This is proposed in relation to the screen industries in Scotland and the designer trades in Glasgow, giving the latter a designated precinct in the city grouped around the new Costume Museum and Fashion Centre.

- Extra jobs in the arts are cheap to provide and there is little inflation risk, which enhances the case for switching existing public spending into this area. Such spending can be targeted towards regions with long-term unemployment.

- Special employment measures could profitably be diverted in some considerable degree to assist with training and helping bodies in the arts rather than to other less rewarding items in the Community Programme.

- Training proposals could be developed, in consultation with the Manpower Services Commission, by Regional Arts Associations, the Area Museum Councils, the Arts Council, the Museums and Galleries Commission, the Crafts Council and the Office of Arts and Libraries.

- Talent lies at the heart of the arts' dynamism, and this feeds into the arts sector and the cultural industries by many complicated routes. Not everything needs public support, but there can be dangers for the system as a whole if training is neglected or particular parts of the system become under-nourished. One of Glasgow's problems, for example, is a draining away of talent to the wider world.

6. *Overseas earnings*

- In film and video the UK has cultural and language advantages and a high reputation in some areas. Considerable growth seems possible, helped by the deregulation of European broadcasting and the integration of the European market.
- A reassessment of the arts in national tourism policy is needed.
- The art trade is threatened by the EEC Seventh Directive which would replace the UK's VAT on margins with a more orthodox tax including VAT on imports. This could promote the export of works of art from Britain and drive a large part of the art market-place to locations outside the EEC. It would be better to extend the UK's special scheme to other countries.
- Encouraging commercial demand for British creative and perfor-ming art is already the work of the British Council. The Council could be encouraged to make regular assessments of its own achievements in this area. If the Council were to adopt an overt promotional role overseas for the arts, its products, performances and services, it would need to develop more fully its relations with the arts scene in the UK. This would also have implications for the training and selection of Council staff.

7. *Extending arts programmes*

- Guidelines for projects need to be developed and - as in the case of Glasgow - related to a wider strategy for improving the regional economy. In Glasgow these guidelines were:

  Will the projects attract extra audiences?

  Will they enhance the prestige of the city and make a mark in international cultural and business circles?

  Will they attract international critical attention?

  Will they stimulate short and medium term cultural tourism?

  Are they consistent with the artistic ambitions and needs of Glasgow's existing arts organisations and their audiences?
- Local strategies should be developed in a way which allows suc-cess to be evaluated. Initiatives should be costed and targeted to show the pay-off in terms of jobs.
- Though museum and gallery spending in Glasgow had a higher economic impact than performing arts, the differences were not large and the two were not rivals but complementary. A broad-based approach encompassing all the arts is recommended.
- Efficient use of existing resources means filling empty seats and gaps in bookings first, so that there is a genuine increase in the marketed output of the arts when new spending is actually under-taken. Successful marketing will be essential.

• New facilities may be essential too - for example Glasgow's new concert hall, which will entice international orchestras and artists. It is important to emphasise that the evidence shows that new facilities both create new audiences and stimulate attendance at established attractions. The evidence from the surveys is that the level of switching from one entertainment to another is low - in other words, putting money into expansion does not mean stealing somebody else's audience.